- Expressions From Eastern England Vol I

Edited by Jessica Woodbridge

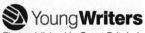 Young**Writers**

First published in Great Britain in 2006 by:
Young Writers
Remus House
Coltsfoot Drive
Peterborough
PE2 9JX
Telephone: 01733 890066
Website: www.youngwriters.co.uk

SB ISBN 1 84602 358 0

Foreword

Young Writers was established in 1991 and has been passionately devoted to the promotion of reading and writing in children and young adults ever since. The quest continues today. Young Writers remains as committed to the fostering of burgeoning poetic and literary talent as ever.

This year's Young Writers competition has proven as vibrant and dynamic as ever and we are delighted to present a showcase of the best poetry from across the UK. Each poem has been carefully selected from a wealth of *Playground Poets* entries before ultimately being published in this, our thirteenth primary school poetry series.

Once again, we have been supremely impressed by the overall high quality of the entries we have received. The imagination, energy and creativity which has gone into each young writer's entry made choosing the best poems a challenging and often difficult but ultimately hugely rewarding task - the general high standard of the work submitted amply vindicating this opportunity to bring their poetry to a larger appreciative audience.

We sincerely hope you are pleased with our final selection and that you will enjoy *Playground Poets - Expressions From Eastern England Vol I* for many years to come.

Contents

Joe Foster (10)   15
Imogen Mintram (9)   15
Ryan Gyles-Brown (10)   15

Bracken Leas School, Brackley
Lewis Marshall, Vincent Sauvan & Emily Collinson (10)   16
James Field (10)   16
Thomas Stephens (10)   17
Oscar Brown   17
Louise Aldus (10)   18
Pollyanna Ford (9)   18
Alex Beckett (9)   19
Ollie Walker   19
Thomas Allen (10)   20
Steven Gibson (10)   20
Annabelle Mann (9)   21
Freddie Ransom (9)   21

Cold Harbour CE School, Milton Keynes
Mollie Procter (8)   21
Ashley Davis (8)   22
Tyler Marshall (8)   22
Matthew Pons (8)   22
Aled Jones (9)   23
Amy Jones (8)   23
Chanelle Nelson (7)   23
George Lee (10)   24
Yazmin Johnson (7)   24
Benjamin Peters (8)   24
Clare Prosser (10)   25
Damilola Obiesesan (9)   25
Elliot Brady (8)   26
Jamie Lee (7)   26
Danika Jackson (11)   26
Alexandra Snihur (9)   27
Ben Rayment (9)   27
Chloe Brooks (10)   27
Chloe Thomson-Smith (9)   28
Alice Barton (9)   28
Thomas Nalton (9)   28
Rheanna O'Neill (9)   29

Luke Holden (9)	29
Danielle Welch (9)	29
Michael Adams (9)	30
Elisabeth Vendelsoe (9)	30
Claire Finney (9)	30
Emily-Kaye Trowell (8)	31
Jade Dawson (9)	31
Hannah Michael (8)	31
Kathrynn Cook (10)	32
Zoe Zukas (10)	32
Nathan Goodenough (8)	32
Gintare Auglyte (10)	33
Fraser Mackay (10)	33
Rehaan Butt (10)	34
Ellie Sturmey (10)	34
Lauren Mathieson (10)	35
Dervla Drinkwater (8)	35
Rebecca Ruggles (10)	36
Faye Devonshire (9)	36
Rosie Barton (10)	37
Robert Gerrard (9)	37
Jasmine Brittain (9)	38
Tunde Awojobi (9)	38
Danial Naqvi (9)	39
Jason Acquaah (10)	39
Jessica Tsoi (11)	40
Yasmine Taherbeigi (10)	40
James Cloke (9)	41
Ryan Johnston (7)	41
Harry Kennedy (8)	41
Bethany Hunt (8)	42
Josh Rodger (7)	42
Adam Goyen (7)	42
James Honhold (9)	43
Jonathan House (9)	43
Marnie-Kate Naughton-Ammon (8)	44
Ryan Smith (9)	44
Hana Robson (9)	45
Karrie Adams (10)	46
Freya Berry (7)	46
Jonathan Osae (9)	47
Sam Ward (9)	47

Hannah Berry (9)   48
Gemma White (9)   48
Ryan Rumsey (9)   49
Melissa Jones (9)   49
Daisy Lynch (9)   50
Emily Stapleton (9)   51
Lydia Mahon (9)   52
Lewis Burt (10)   52
David Orange (9)   52
Charlotte Ring (9)   53
Wesley Sherratt (10)   53
Taylor Stewart (10)   54
Aimée Lewington (10)   54
Chris Showler (10)   55
Zoe Morris (9)   55
Jake Tighe (10)   55
Sam Jordan (9)   56
Yaw Ofosu (9)   56

Denfield Park Junior School, Rushden
Ben Percy (9)   56
Elenore Linsell (9)   57
Jodie Pitfield (9)   57
Emily McAlwane (9)   57
Sasha Harris (9)   58

Gayhurst School, Gerrards Cross
Max Rolfe (9)   58
Alex Mann (9)   59
Matthew O'Regan (10)   59
Amit Patel (11)   60
Max Johnston (10)   60
Parus Nischal (10)   61
Christopher Katanchian (10)   61
Toby Foster (10)   62
Sam Zatland (10)   62
Harrypal Panesar (10)   63
Jack Baker (10)   63
Adam Jackson (9)   64
Ryan Campkin (10)   64
Christopher Neophytou (9)   65

Bradley Stone (9)	65
Robert Sutherland (9)	66
Hugo Davis (10)	66
Daniel Steele (10)	66
Samuel Millard (10)	67
Julian Knoester (10)	67
Bertie Martine (10)	67
George Lawley (8)	68
Joshua Kirby (8)	68
Matthew Pugh (9)	69
Alex Deninson (8)	69
Conor Arnot (8)	70
Charlie West (10)	70
Brodie Steele (9)	71
Ross Buckley (8)	71
Oliver Levi (8)	72
Andile Mathebula (8)	72
Siddharth Saraogi (8)	73
Charles Galligan (9)	73
Connor Broadley (10)	74
Oliver Phipps (8)	74
Cameron Conn (8)	75
Joshua Ferguson (8)	75
Jack Butler (9)	76
Elliot Van Barthold (9)	76
Aarib Khan (9)	77
William Bowen (9)	77
George Nolan (10)	78
Joseph Bull (8)	78
Sean Gray (9)	79
Kayal Patel (7)	79
Barnaby Wilson (10)	80
Callum James (9)	80
Timothy Hatton (9)	80
Harish Malhi (10)	81
Thomas Mockridge (9)	81
Seyvan Kellay (9)	81
Chris Hayes (10)	82
Joshua Pinchess (10)	83
Paddy Keogh (8)	83
William Martin (8)	84
Edwin Grimster (8)	84

Ben Eastwood (8)	85
James Liveing (8)	85
Craig Baillie (10)	86
Harry Cruickshank (10)	86
Peter Illingworth (11)	87
Ben Reeves (9)	87

Laxton Junior School, Oundle

Ellie Raby-Smith (10)	88
Aditya Shukla (10)	88
Kiristina Cowley (11)	89
Joshua Green (7)	89
Eliza Burgess (9)	90
Phoebe McCurdy (9)	90
Zulfiqar-E-Aly Dooley Kachra (9)	91
Freya Grayson (7)	91
Kayla Borley (8)	92
Ben Amps (8)	92
Alexandra Tonks (10)	93
Francesca Hooper (7)	93
Elizabeth Farrell (8)	94
Tessa Berridge (10)	94
Mary Bletsoe (7)	95
Ben Learoyd (7)	95
Chloe Van Slyke (8)	96
Amrish Rajdev (10)	96
Lauren Ferdinand (8)	96
Shalinie Sriemevan (10)	97
Molly Clayton (9)	97
Katie Orr (9)	98
Anna Pathak (7)	98
William Sly (7)	99
Lily Clayton (10)	99
Georgina Illingworth (10)	100
Angus Murphy (10)	100
Jesse Chambers (10)	101
Eve Poulter (10)	101

Meadowside Junior School, Kettering

Reece Coles (9)	102
Demi Chapman (9)	102

Ellie Buckby (10)	103
Jordan Coles (10)	103
Zoe Gunter (9)	104
Richard Ashcroft (10)	104
Kimberley Kingsnorth (10)	105
Georgia Harrison (10)	105
Tasha McIntyre (10)	106
Josh Hicks (10)	106
Charlotte Ashworth (10)	107

Putteridge Junior School, Luton

Bethany Clifton (9)	107
Thomas Fox-Johnson (8)	108
Angel George (8)	108
Amy Parkins (11)	109
Samantha Gray (8)	109
Kavi Raval (10)	110
Emily Goddard (7)	111
Laxman Godhania (10)	111
Hayley Watson (10)	112
Danielle Gooch (8)	112
Matthew Dawson (11)	113
Bethany Freeman (9)	113
Alice Kiss (10)	114
Hannah Lake (10)	114
William Shadbolt (8)	115
Eleanor Hudson (9)	115
Abigail Parry (11)	116
Matthew Dimmock (8)	116
Sammy-Jo McGrath (11)	117
Samantha Weaver (8)	117
Manisha Bajaj (10)	118
Kim Hughes (8)	118
Nina Kiva (8)	119
Ellie Chittenden (8)	119
Megan Close (10)	120
Katie Riviere (8)	120
Charlie Pepper (10)	121
Hannah Kiss (9)	121
Matthew Chamberlain (8)	122
Jamie Loveday (9)	122

Katy Risbridger (10)   123
Bradley Andrews (8)   123
Sam Glenister (9)   124
Daniel Auburn (8)   124
Oliver Goddard (9)   125
Helena Gookey (9)   126
Stephanie Little (10)   127
Louie Penfold (10)   128
Michaella Beckwith (10)   128
Joe Tucker (8)   129
Amy Pollard (10)   129
Michael Jones (10)   130
Pratik Shah (8)   130
Alisha Seera (8)   131
Lauren James (8)   131
Alex Hayward (8)   131
Jack Hattle (9)   132
Amy Gardner (9)   132
Yasmin Kreft (8)   133
Sophie Webb (10)   133
Kellyanne Batchelor (10)   134
Harkirit Rayatt (8)   134
Sam Ferrell (10)   135
Sophie Smith (8)   135
Louis Horan (10)   136
Adam Joyce (8)   136
Amber Godfrey (8)   137
Jay Clarke (8)   137
Sam Gale (11)   138
Sebastian Cooper (8)   138
Kayley-Anne Lee (10)   139
Miraj Shah (8)   139
Sophie Risbridger (8)   140
Russell Attwood (10)   140
William Finnie (11) & Miheer Soni (10)   141
Kendall Bull (10) & Lewis Hills (10)   142
Lewis Synan-Jones (10)   143
Megan Ward (10)   143
Mandla Bandama (11)   144
Patrick Frater-Loughlin (10)   145
Ross Arnold (8)   146
David Lapushner (10)   146

Rhys O'Nions (10)   147
Harry Burnham (8)   147
Raja Birring (10)   148
Ashleigh Bowler (8)   148
Charlie Jeycock (8)   149
George Harris (8)   149
Alanta Castleman (8)   149
Ashley Purdy (8)   150
Rebecca Carter (8)   150
Mohammed Ibara Ali Razaq (9)   151
Bradley Essex (8)   151
Yasser Thamer (8)   152

St Mary Magdalene Catholic Primary School, Milton Keynes

Paul Goddard (9)   152
Drew Hennessy (10)   152
Melanie Commey (9)   153
Chelsea Coltart (9)   153
Amber Sayles (9)   153
Oyinkansola Fowowe (9)   154
Kaiya Feeney (9)   154
Bethany Conway (9)   154
Fraser Green (9)   155
Jonathan Vines (9)   155
Alex Miles (9)   155
Katie Rance (9)   156
Katy Worton (9)   156
Erin Soden (9)   156
Jessica Hipwell (10)   157
Benita Cappellano (9)   157
Lauren Joy (9)   158
Maxwell Graham (9)   158
Jordan Keating (9)   158
Dylan Joseph (9)   159
Joanna Lloyd Knibbs (9)   159
Nathaniel Graham (9)   159
Alice Davies (11)   160
Danielle Lauderdale (8)   160
Sophie Guiry (9)   160
Emilio Baqueiro (10)   161
Patricia Ogunjobi (10)   161

Derryn Hudson (10)	177
Jodie Towell (10)	177
Hibak Jama (10)	177
Khama Banda (10)	178
Callum Spray (10)	178
Vicki Vernon (10)	178
Scott Culley (10)	178
Kalhun Carr (10)	179
Jordan Noon (10)	179
Rhiannon Fox (10)	179
Chloe Duff (9)	180
Danielle Harrison (9)	180
Joshua Clements (9)	180
Tyler Cutts (8)	181
Gabrielle Jane Beasley (10)	181
Kelly Nicole Hutson (9)	181
Elizabeth Mulcahy (8)	182
Arthur Woolley (8)	182
Ciaran Clark (10)	182
Corey Ringer (10)	183
Kristina Kent-Rettig (9)	183
Dane Morgan (9)	184
Gemma Argent (9)	184
Jamielee Tucker Spiers (9)	184
Sarah Roberts (10)	185
Saffron Lucas (9)	185
Wesley Brown (9)	186
Charlyn Kumadi (9)	186

Weedon Bec Primary School, Northampton

Alice Walker (7)	186
Emily Conder (7)	187
India Daniels (7)	187
Alice Bendy (8)	188
Joseph Gilbert (7)	188
Alexandra Holyoak (9)	188
Calvin Thorogood (8)	189
Ashley Rawlings (9)	189
Jessica Browne (9)	189
Colleen Hogan (7)	190
Cally Brooks (7)	190

Alice Sayward (7)	190
Chelsea Marks (7)	191
Samantha Nicholls-Kidner (9)	191
Georgina Holyoak (7)	191
Laura Smith (7)	192
Francesca Sorrentino (7)	192
Rhys Watkins (7)	192
Dominic Knight (9)	193
Rhiannon Kay (8)	193
Mark Fennell (10)	194
Austin Wilde (11)	194
Alex Horner (9)	194
Hannah Barnes (8)	195
Jorja Mills (8)	195
Georgina Laye (9)	196
Lauren Gilbert (9)	196
Kayleigh Marks (10)	197
Courtney Hogan (9)	197
Emmah Suhail (10)	198
Amy Pask (10)	198
Daniella Day (9)	199

Wellingborough Preparatory School, Wellingborough

Alex Freeman-Hall (9)	199
Issy Tai (10)	200
Max Armstrong (10)	200
Alex Lill (10)	201
Ralph Titmuss (11)	202
Charlie Oliver Miller (10)	203
William Aitken (11)	204
Rory Millett (11)	204
Ben Squire (10)	205
Lydia Smart (9)	205
Ruth Simone Sherry (8)	206

The Poems

Football Match

The referee blew his whistle
As we played Scotland who were wearing the thistle.

We pushed through on goal
The defence left a gaping hole.

The crowd screamed so loud
It made us so proud.

I struck the ball into the net
Which made me win my five-pound bet!

Kirby Parrish (10)
All Saints' Primary School, March

Mum

Mum, you are like dark chocolate melting on my ice cream
Because you bought me ice cream when I was sad.
I think of you as the stars shining in the sky
Because when I look up I see a shape and it looks like you.
I think of you in my feelings
I said I love you and I always will.
You are like the pink sky at night
And that reminds me of you.

Evie Cox (8)
All Saints' Primary School, March

Butterflies

Butterflies, butterflies fly around
Butterflies, butterflies make a sound
Butterflies, butterflies by the countryside
Butterflies, butterflies by my side.

Chloe Spencer (7)
All Saints' Primary School, March

Summer

As the sky brightens up for summer,
Blazing down on us the sun gets burnt itself,
The smiling sun greets us like a member of its family,
With the biggest smile on its face.

The flowers sing along to songs I put on,
The hot air breezes through the houses.

One tiny cloud disappears,
As every flower dances around,
The day feels cosier
After a day of bright sunshine.

Niomi Stromberg (10)
All Saints' Primary School, March

Mum

You are the pink of my roses
You are the rhythm of flying like a bird
You are the tomato on my pizza
You are the bubbles in my 7Up
You are the cotton of my skirts and tops
You are the shops of London
You are the surprise of my Christmas.

Chanice Cooke (8)
All Saints' Primary School, March

Winter

Winter is coming through the year.
Snow is falling like a skydiver diving from one-hundred feet.
Hailstones are barging into people like someone in a rush.
The rain pitter-patters on the window like a heart beating.
Animals don't like winter, neither do I.

Rachael Harwin (10)
All Saints' Primary School, March

Double Bass

A double bass is a funny old instrument.
It looks like a very pointed arrow in a vast stomach.
Its curves are like green hills in the countryside.
It has an enormous fat belly like a stupendous giant.
When you bow it, it sounds like a screaming opera singer.
But when you pluck it the strings break in two.
Yes, the double bass is a lovely laughable instrument!

James Abbott (10)
All Saints' Primary School, March

Flowers

Your petals bloom like a starfish,
Your scent tickles my nose,
The bees settle on you and collect your pollen
You must be thirsty sitting there in the sun,
I'll water you when the day is done.

Stephanie Collins (10)
All Saints' Primary School, March

Autumn

Autumn is amber, crimson and chestnut-brown leaves.
Autumn is floating, fluttering, falling leaves.
Autumn is purple blackberries, blue blueberries and pink raspberries.
Autumn is pinecones, acorns and hazelnuts.
Autumn is one of my favourite seasons
Because I love picking berries and collecting leaves.
Autumn is cloudy days.
Autumn is wrapping up nice and warm.
Autumn is getting ready for winter.

Sarah Wheatley (9)
Baston CE Primary School, Baston

Hey Diddle Diddle

(Based on the nursery rhyme 'Hey Diddle Diddle')

Hey diddle diddle,
The cat worked out a riddle
The cow tripped up a baboon.
The little pig oinked to see such fun
And the mouse said, 'I'll see you soon.'

Hey diddle diddle
The goat's playing the fiddle
He's playing a very good tune.
The horse said, 'Hello' and the pig turned yellow
And he said, 'I will see you next June.'

Hey diddle diddle
The sheep's in the middle
The fish has just reached the moon.
The little bear jumped and came back down
And the fox ran away with the spoon.

Laura Baker (9)
Baston CE Primary School, Baston

Christmas

Christmas is fun
Christmas is great
Christmas is good on every date
Christmas is fun, baking a cake.

Christmas is really cool
Christmas is really fun playing in the snow
Christmas is cool with family coming over for Christmas dinner
Christmas is not always snowy.

Christmas is chilly and cold
Christmas is cool seeing your stocking full with presents
Christmas is fun opening my presents
Christmas is the *best day ever.*

Charlotte Moore (8)
Baston CE Primary School, Baston

Writing

The phone is ringing, 'I'm coming' I say,
'Hello who is it? Is it my brother?'
It's my young brother from the USA.

The snow is falling, it is now Christmas,
I can't wait till I open the presents,
The Christmas tree is beautiful and bright.

The stream is running past,
Boats are putting up their masts
No one wants to be the last.

The teacher's waiting,
This lesson she hates
She's hesitating.

Danielle Lea (8)
Baston CE Primary School, Baston

The Invasion

UFOs and aliens
Attacking from the dark sky
Heading to Earth

Firing triggers
Upon the steaming island
Coming forth to kill

Gaining speed upon Earth
Death is upon Earth today
So we fight for life

As a last resort
We come back in victory
With our heads held high.

Max Morgan-Kay (10)
Baston CE Primary School, Baston

Seasons

Spring
All the trees are blossoming
Leaves are turning green
Sheep are having baby lambs
And birds are being seen.

Summer
Playing on the beaches
The scorching hot sun
Sunbathing in the garden
And having lots of fun.

Autumn
Jumping in the crunching leaves
The foggy chilly mornings
All the geese are flying south
And the weather is giving us warnings.

Winter
Waking up to snow falling
Children making snowmen
People like me in scarves and hats
And a hedgehog in its den.

Georgina Hall (8)
Baston CE Primary School, Baston

The Four Seasons

Spring
Leaves starting to turn green
Birds starting to be seen
Baby animals being born
Cows yes but not bulls with horns.

Summer
Sea back and beaches
Water gone from ditches
Children building castles and moats
No more winter coats.

Autumn
Leaves falling off trees
Brown, gold, orange, not green
Squirrels looking for nuts
School starting, paper cuts.

Winter
No green grass to mow
Children playing in the snow
Christmas Day and Christmas Eve
Just Father Christmas, no thieves.

James McCrae (8)
Baston CE Primary School, Baston

Space

What planet do we live on?
Is it . . .
Mars
Mercury
Jupiter
Or Uranus?
No, so
What planet do we live on?
Is it . . .
Venus
Pluto
Saturn
Or Neptune?
No, so
What planet do we live on?
Earth!

Jenny Hutchins (9)
Baston CE Primary School, Baston

My Little Doggies - Haikus

Patch, fluffy, bright eyes
Running, jumping in the park,
Happy, tail wagging.

Frolic, black and white,
Jumping up and down all day,
On a sunny day.

Tawny playing out,
A tiny little rascal,
Covered in brown mud.

Dixie huddled up,
Snuggled in my lovely bed,
Tiny as can be.

Victoria Kong (8)
Baston CE Primary School, Baston

Haikus

The deadly night comes
Bats come out to fly around
Screeching and shouting

The teacher's waiting
For the children's attention
But no attention

A big rainforest
Is getting attacked down where
The animals are

Zombies awake and
Go into town and destroy
And break all of it.

Alex Weston (9)
Baston CE Primary School, Baston

Harvest

Harvest time comes once a year,
Hallowe'en is creeping near,
People gather in their crops,
But come sunset the rushing stops.
Food is gathered, fruit and berries,
Ripe, flavoured redcurrants and juicy cherries.
Someone will have a wonderful feast,
Whilst others, their crops have withered, deceased.
If you are having a harvest meal,
Just remember how those others will feel.

Elleanor Crouch (11)
Beaupré Community Primary School, Wisbech

The Seaside

One day I went to the seaside,
A brilliant day I had
It was a long time since I had been to the seaside
So the day made me ever so glad.
I strolled along the prom very slowly
Taking in all of the sights
Children on the beach happily playing
While the parents kept them in their sight.
Some were looking for seashells
While others swam with delight.
Some making fabulous sandcastles
With flags, colourful and bright.
The day was almost over
Everyone getting ready for home
Two things we hadn't got round to
Were hot doughnuts and an ice cream cone.
As we reached home and I finally fell into my little snug bed
With all the beautiful memories floating around in my head.

Amber Farrow (10)
Beaupré Community Primary School, Wisbech

Harvest Time

H arvest time comes once a year
A nd farmers start to collect their food.
R eaping crops across the lands.
V egetables are nice and fully grown.
E aster comes before harvest.
S pecial vegetables are grown for harvest.
T he vegetables come in all different sizes.

Natasha Scott (10)
Beaupré Community Primary School, Wisbech

The Zoo

The zoo has all the greatest animals
From elephants to ants in the insect house.
The giraffes can see the whole zoo
While the penguins can only see people
Staring and pointing through the glass.
In the monkey enclosure the orang-utans swing around
While the chimpanzees look after cute clingy babies, they're so small.
In the insect and reptile house the ants carry the leaves up a rope
And the tarantulas stare out scarily
But scariest of all, the alligator, *argh!*

Phoebe Langer (10)
Blakesley CE Primary School, Towcester

Dogs

Fluffy, loud, playful and active
That's what dogs are all about.

Big, small, lazy at home
Lots of dogs are just like that.

Loving, caring but angry at thieves
That's the kind of dog I want.

Playful, happy, Man's best friend
That's what a loving dog is like.

Charlie Hackett (10)
Blakesley CE Primary School, Towcester

On The Christmas Tree

Red and blue baubles on a Christmas tree.
Lights lighting up the cold room on a Christmas tree.
Sparkles on a Christmas tree with a fairy on top.
Merry Christmas, merry Christmas *everyone!*

Eleanor Broadfield (9)
Blakesley CE Primary School, Towcester

BMXs

GT a fast bike used for jumps and it comes down with a thump.
If you go off a kerb try not to get disturbed,
Because if you fall off or crash, your bike will go up in a smash!

Huffy is an off-road bike used for doing radical stunts,
It's not used for big fat jumps.
I'll give it a ten out of ten,
I might hire one and have a ride again.

Mongoose is a bike for hills,
After a while your head kills.
You go upright, left and down,
If you fall off you will break your crown.
I came off a rock,
'Oh no I can't stop!'

Bradley Harper (9)
Blakesley CE Primary School, Towcester

Best Friends

B est friends for life.
E xciting friends do everything together.
S ensible friends never break up.
T heir best sport is cricket!

F unky friends are really cool.
R eally good friends are really fancy.
I nteresting friends can be fun.
E xcellent friends are for life.
N ice friends are friends for life.
D ancing friends are special.
S ome friends break up at times.

Abigail Chambers (10)
Blakesley CE Primary School, Towcester

Who Am I?

I have long whiskers coming off my face.
I also have big blue eyes looking out at you.
My eyes help me to see in the dark.
I have a nose to help me sniff you out.
Do you know who I am?
Because I want a hug.

I have four legs, yet I can't walk on two.
I also have one tail that swings when I'm angry.
I sleep on your lap.
I purr when you tickle me under my chin.
I miaow loudly when you stand on my tail!
Do you know who I am?
Because I want a hug!

A: Cat.

Caroline Rodhouse (10)
Blakesley CE Primary School, Towcester

Best Friend

B est friends forever.
E xciting friends are fun.
S cary stories are their favourite.
T heir best sport is basketball.

F riends can be funny.
R eally cool friends are nice.
I nteresting friends for life.
E agles are their favourite birds.
N ice friends forever.
D Js they are.
S ensible friends never break up!

Christopher Purr (10)
Blakesley CE Primary School, Towcester

Cars

Range Rovers, Land Rovers and Ferraris,
Marcos Mantis, Porsches and Maclarens,
Fords, BMWs and Mercedes.
Dragsters, top fuel and funny cars
VW Beetles, Passats and Golfs,
Nissans, Toyotas and Citroens,
Subarus, Mitsubishis, Audis and Renaults.
Dodge Vipers, Chevrolet Corvettes,
Fiats, Vauxhalls and more,
Jaguars, Aston Martins and Noble M400.

Adam Jones (10)
Blakesley CE Primary School, Towcester

Dogs

Loud, quiet, funny too,
Active for walks,
But lazy at home.

There are big ones, small ones,
Fat ones, skinny ones, fluffy ones too.

Bites, licks, jumps, plays.
It's Man's best friend!

Ross Duggan (10)
Blakesley CE Primary School, Towcester

Chocolate Cake

Chocolate cake is great!
With rainbow sprinkles on top,
Caramel oozing out of the middle,
When you cut the cake it's a fiddle!
But! when you taste it,
It's totally different!

Beth Mintram (9)
Blakesley CE Primary School, Towcester

BMXs

Going up a half-pipe
On a great GT

Going up a quarter pipe
On a Super Mongoose.

Going up a ramp
On a Wicked Huffy.

Landing on the
Landing ramp hopefully.

Giving backies down a hill
On the best bikes, BMXs.

Joe Foster (10)
Blakesley CE Primary School, Towcester

Christmas

Bright lights make the city shine
Happy faces everywhere
Warm fire heats the room
Merry music on the radio
Pretty decorations on the tree
Yummy food on the table
Spectacular gifts,
Fun, fun, fun!

Imogen Mintram (9)
Blakesley CE Primary School, Towcester

Cars

C ars getting cleaned by the owners.
A wesome Porsches and Ferraris racing on the track.
R acing cars in the garage that are getting repaired.
S parkly paint the colour of blood.

Ryan Gyles-Brown (10)
Blakesley CE Primary School, Towcester

Apple

What am I?
Smooth apples hanging about on chocolate branches,
Surrounded by verdant leaves
Swaying around in a slippery rosy red coat is a healthy fruit.

What can I feel?
Sapphire raindrops falling silently,
Splashing on the crimson apples.
Gentle breeze brushing against the ripened pears.
Warm sun gleaming on the morning dew.
Fresh cool evening air flowing over
Smooth mahogany conkers on the ground.

What can I see?
Playful children bounding through the crispy autumn leaves.
Misty grey sky covered with slate-coloured clouds.
A farmer strolling through the swaying topaz corn.

Lewis Marshall, Vincent Sauvan & Emily Collinson (10)
Bracken Leas School, Brackley

Corn

What can I see?
I can see my fellow corn,
Sitting in their little coats,
Next to us a field of oats,
The sun beaming down on us.

What can I hear?
I can hear the wind rushing by,
I then heard the sound of rain and then it came,
Falling on me colour of flame,
Then it stopped and all sound faded.

What can I feel?
I can feel a bug crawling on me,
I can hear the wind in a nearby tree,
A sigh of relief as the harvester passes by me,
Maybe next time it will be me being picked up, *gulp!*

James Field (10)
Bracken Leas School, Brackley

The Legendary Battle

In my castle of spiky green
I see an opening
I look at myself and think
Is it my turn to join the legendary battle
Against another conker like me?
And now I see blue sky
And hear the sound of roaring cars
I feel a jerk and hear a sound
As I fall onto the green grass of today.
The whole of my castle breaks
And I see a shadow on the ground
A monster picks me up and takes me
Away and prepares me for the battle
I always dreamed of.
I see my enemy and strengthen my defences
I go in and win the battle on my first hit
I may feel dizzy and the world is spinning
But I feel a champion
And prepare myself for my next encounter, with death.

Thomas Stephens (10)
Bracken Leas School, Brackley

Coral

Oh coral is a beautiful thing
You can dive right down and snap a piece off.
It glitters in the sunlight and shines in the moon
But it is a sharp rock.
Fish hide in its slanty surface with a thousand stars in each piece.
It is violet and sometimes shiny pink.
Fish hide in its glossy surface
So that they can hide from predators and pounce on their prey.
Coral is like an old man's hand that has been crippled by time.
I love coral!

Oscar Brown
Bracken Leas School, Brackley

Dangling Free

What can I see?
Here I am dangling free,
From my branch I can see,
On the opposite tree,
An apple smiling at me.

What can I hear?
The wind rushing by,
Birds twittering in the sky,
A child beginning to cry.

What can I feel?
The wind rushing past,
Children climbing fast,
Birds hopping on my branches,
Sharing out their insect catches,
But you haven't guessed who I am,
As all the doors shut,
I'm all alone,
A hazelnut!

Louise Aldus (10)
Bracken Leas School, Brackley

The Panther

Swoop and strike
Darting for its prey
Leaping and sprinting
But it just wants to play!
King of the jungle.

Chase and chew
Knows just what to do
Sound an ear-splitting roar
Panther!

Pollyanna Ford (9)
Bracken Leas School, Brackley

Curious Creature

At dusk, emerging from the leaf litter at the
end of the garden is an animal . . .

The animal moves
with the domino effect.
It has one thousand
limbs.
The animal is one
metre long, so it is
not an insect.
It squirts out gallons of
smelly juice at a
centipede ready for
lunch.
With feelers as long
as lengths of string
and a body quite like a
small snake.
It's a slippery, slimy,
gruesome, grimy,
disgusting, dirty
Millipede!

Alex Beckett (9)
Bracken Leas School, Brackley

Untitled

Slimy tentacles,
Slimy head,
Sharp beak
Black inky smokescreen
Grey, dull, thick skin
Tentacles like tyres
Swimming elegantly
Big muscular body
Massive round head
Colossal circular eyes.

Ollie Walker
Bracken Leas School, Brackley

The Poem Of A Blackberry

What can I see?
I live in a kingdom of spikes,
With only my fellow blackberries for company,
I often see ravenous people coming my way,
Armed with baskets and plastic containers,
Coming to pick me.

What can I hear?
I can hear children's gleeful shouts,
Of getting a ripe blackberry,
Aeroplanes passing over me,
Making a loud noise in the sky.

What can I feel?
I can feel the gentle breeze,
Of the wind blowing on me,
The vibration of my bush,
As a boy bends down to pick me,
My life is about to come to an end,
As I feel myself being put into a pie.

Thomas Allen (10)
Bracken Leas School, Brackley

Colossal Corn

Here I am resting in the field,
Swinging in the breeze.
I can see fields of fabric patterns,
Glistening sky and chalky stripes.
I hear birds singing in the wind,
Welcoming the day as it begins.
Jet planes roaring,
As they soar to their destination.
I feel like nothing I've felt before,
The heat of the sun,
And the freshness of the breeze.
I am ready to be picked,
And to be stored.

Steven Gibson (10)
Bracken Leas School, Brackley

The Snake

Slippery, slimy, sliding, suspicious, sly snake
With smooth, glossy skin as shiny as glass
Winding in-between sharp rocks.
Eyes like stars glittering in the moonlight,
Body skimming the leafy ground.
Tongue flicking in and out sensing heat,
Tail swishing like a whip.
Fangs like grappling hooks,
Silently darting beneath a root
Grab the mouse! Rip the mouse!
Tear the mouse! Snap! Crunch! Swallow . . . *gone!*

Annabelle Mann (9)
Bracken Leas School, Brackley

Fairground Ride

There was a roller coaster that had a colossal corkscrew
That shot past me at lightning fast speeds,
Darted down the death defying drops
And glided through the vertical v-turns
And then it flew through, spiralling, spinning, round and round
Then vertically coming to the ground.

Freddie Ransom (9)
Bracken Leas School, Brackley

Apples

Apples are juicy and yummy in my tummy.
Round and fat.
Crunchy and solid.
Juice dripping from my apple
Red and yellow blend in my apple.

Mollie Procter (8)
Cold Harbour CE School, Milton Keynes

Pomegranates

Pomegranates are mouth-watering,
Luscious and sweet.
Not sour, not bitter but sweet.
They're also juicy and lovely.
They're the best fruit you will ever taste.
A pomegranate is the best.
You won't love it till you try it.
So get one today and try it.

Ashley Davis (8)
Cold Harbour CE School, Milton Keynes

Pomegranate

Juice of wonders
Lovely taste of dreams
Water moving everywhere
Scrumptious taste of dreams
Seeds wrapped up by soury flavours
Round like an apple
Colours like an apple
You're dreaming you're eating a pomegranate.

Tyler Marshall (8)
Cold Harbour CE School, Milton Keynes

Apples

Apples are splendid to eat.
Colourful when they fall off the tree.
Scrumptious in your belly.
Sweet and juicy.
Delicious and green if you cut them half.

Matthew Pons (8)
Cold Harbour CE School, Milton Keynes

What Makes Me Happy?

What makes me happy . . .
Is when my brother tickles me.
Is watching funny movies and programmes.
Is going on holiday.
Is going to a birthday party.
Is Christmas Day, because I get to open the presents.
Is going to my friend's house.
Is going to football practise.
Is Pancake Day.
I like this poem.

Aled Jones (9)
Cold Harbour CE School, Milton Keynes

Carrot

C arrot, carrot, juicy and crunchy
A nd munchy too
R eally tasty
R eally good for you
O range and healthy as can be
T ake a bite and see.

Amy Jones (8)
Cold Harbour CE School, Milton Keynes

Carrots

Carrots are crunchy
Orange and bushy at the top
Tasty and healthy for your cholesterol and energy
Small, big, take a big bite
It will help you
Bumpy and smooth.

Chanelle Nelson (7)
Cold Harbour CE School, Milton Keynes

My Cats

My cats are good pets
They're big and fluffy,
They're ginger and black
And they're really funny.

They sleep on my bed
They eat things outside,
They're always hungry
And sleep all day.

They eat all the chicken
They eat a lot of food
They play fight with each other
And play with small balls.

George Lee (10)
Cold Harbour CE School, Milton Keynes

Cauliflower

It's bumpy, white, green and crunchy
And spotty and very tasty
Solid, hard and leafy
Cold and makes you hungry.

Yazmin Johnson (7)
Cold Harbour CE School, Milton Keynes

Leaf

Flexible, crunchy, veiny, oval
Leafy, leafy, crunchy leaf.
Colourful, bright, green lump
Leafy, leafy crunch.

Benjamin Peters (8)
Cold Harbour CE School, Milton Keynes

Kittens

Kittens are sweet
Cute as can be
Fluffy little coats
And little mischief makers.

They climb up on your legs
Jump out of odd places
They play hide-and-seek
And then they sleep.

When they awaken
They're ready to fight
They jump up and down
They play cat and mouse.

They creep up from behind
And chase each other round
They try to get their tails
Oh what joy they are to be around.

Clare Prosser (10)
Cold Harbour CE School, Milton Keynes

What Makes Me Happy . . .

Is going to a relaxing beach.
Is my friends when they are happy.
Is Christmas.
Is choosing what I want for my birthday.
Is being with my family.
Is when it snows.
Is singing.
Is dancing.
Is really looking fantastic all the time.
Is going to brilliant houses.

Damilola Obiesesan (9)
Cold Harbour CE School, Milton Keynes

Untitled

Big, hard like a rock.
I love conkers, yes I do.
The shell's hard, sharp, solid.
I love conkers, yes I do.
White on top, brown on the bottom, all the colours.
I love conkers, yes I do.
On the inside all green and damp.
I love conkers, yes I do.
When two go together, *bang, crash, crack!*
I love conkers except for when they break.

Elliot Brady (8)
Cold Harbour CE School, Milton Keynes

Conkers

Conkers are bumpy and fat and prickly
Conkers are smooth and cracked
Conkers are hard and dark and brown
Conkers are shiny and greasy
Conkers are nice and I like conkers
Conkers can be green and new
Conkers are spiky and very small and big.

Jamie Lee (7)
Cold Harbour CE School, Milton Keynes

Sandy

We have a dog called Sandy
She walks really bandy,
Her face is so sweet,
You can give her a treat,
Her tail is a stump
That looks like a bump!

Danika Jackson (11)
Cold Harbour CE School, Milton Keynes

Conkers

Bashing, crashing, tough and spotty.
Big, brown conker solid and rocky.
Shiny, spotty, indestructible.
Horse chestnut, conker shell spiky as a hedgehog.
Chocolaty coloured conker, all of a sudden, *crash!*
The conker's falling from the tree,
It's calling you and it's calling me!
Damp, crooked, bumpy,
Suddenly . . . it breaks!

Alexandra Snihur (9)
Cold Harbour CE School, Milton Keynes

What Makes Me Sad . . .

Is having no fun with my friends when I am down.
Is having no one to care for me.
Is people making fun of me.
Is people kicking, punching and pinching me.
Is seeing people suffer.
Is having no friends at all.
Is seeing drunk people attacking other people.

Ben Rayment (9)
Cold Harbour CE School, Milton Keynes

Rocket!

A rocket flies in the sky
All the planets pass by!
Sky, asteroids and stars
Milky Way and Mars.
It really is an amazing place,
How I wish I could go up in space.

Chloe Brooks (10)
Cold Harbour CE School, Milton Keynes

What Makes Me Sad

What makes me sad is when people talk about my grandad Cyril
Who died before I was born.
And it is when people talk about Peter and take pity on him
And then I get all lonely;
What makes me sad is when I hear that Jasmine is going back
                                                    to New Zealand
And when a friend and another friend fight.
What makes you feel sad?

Chloe Thomson-Smith (9)
Cold Harbour CE School, Milton Keynes

On My Own

On my own I couldn't play Pictionary or tag.
On my own a see-saw is always down.
On my own I can't give a home-made friendship bracelet.
On my own I can't have fun on my birthday.
On my own I can't make a friendship on holiday.
On my own I can't play swing ball.

Alice Barton (9)
Cold Harbour CE School, Milton Keynes

On My Own

On my own a see-saw is always down.
On my own I couldn't play Pictionary or tag.
On my own a game of Quasar would be pointless.
On my own feelings and secrets would be sealed up.
On my own no one's there to push you on the swing.
On my own I couldn't go on holiday.

Thomas Nalton (9)
Cold Harbour CE School, Milton Keynes

On My Own

On my own a see-saw is always down!
On my own I couldn't play Pictionary or tag!
On my own I can't smile!
On my own I feel the sun is not shining on me!
On my own I can't make friendship bracelets!
On my own I can't tell my ideas and secrets!

Rheanna O'Neill (9)
Cold Harbour CE School, Milton Keynes

What Makes Me Sad

What makes me sad . . .
Is when bad things happen.
Is when I get a yellow or a red card at football.
Is when I break my bones.
Is when my pets or relatives die.
Is when I hurt myself on holiday.

Luke Holden (9)
Cold Harbour CE School, Milton Keynes

On My Own

On my own the see-saw is always down.
On my own I can't play tag.
On my own I can't share a laugh.
On my own the swing wouldn't get pushed.
On my own there's nobody to comfort me.
On my own I wouldn't be happy.

Danielle Welch (9)
Cold Harbour CE School, Milton Keynes

What Makes Me Happy

What makes me happy . . .
Is reading a funny book.
Is watching my little brother running round the house naked.
Is beating my dad at Age of Empires.
Is eating pizza for tea.
Is using my little brother as a pillow.
Is Mum making chocolate cake.
Is lobbing snowballs at my little brother.
Is watching the movie 'Madagascar'.
Is biking round Willen Lake.
Is having a lie-in on a Saturday.
Is beating Rob at roller rock.

Michael Adams (9)
Cold Harbour CE School, Milton Keynes

What Makes Me Sad

What makes me sad is having nobody to play with all day.
What makes me sad is when my dad goes all over the world
And isn't here on my birthday.
What makes me sad is saying goodbye to my friends
When they leave the school.
What makes me sad is coming back from holiday.

Elisabeth Vendelsoe (9)
Cold Harbour CE School, Milton Keynes

On My Own

On my own a see-saw is always down.
On my own I couldn't play Pictionary or tag.
On my own I can't share a laugh.
On my own the swing wouldn't get pushed.
On my own nobody to comfort me.
On my own I wouldn't be happy.

Claire Finney (9)
Cold Harbour CE School, Milton Keynes

Pumpkin

My pumpkin is a bright orange colour,
Inside beautiful tastes that you could never imagine,
You should try it,
You would like it,
Yummy, scrummy pumpkin.
Soft flesh, soft and smooth,
Make a triangle for its nose,
Two smaller triangles for eyes and
One big goofy smile for a Hallowe'en pumpkin!
The pips are small and very hard,
The juices are immaculate,
The flesh is all sloppy.
My orange pumpkin!

Emily-Kaye Trowell (8)
Cold Harbour CE School, Milton Keynes

On My Own

On my own a see-saw is always down.
On my own I couldn't play Pictionary or tag.
On my own I couldn't have a birthday.
On my own I couldn't play out.
On my own I couldn't share secrets with friends.
On my own I couldn't make a team.
On my own I couldn't send postcards to anyone.

Jade Dawson (9)
Cold Harbour CE School, Milton Keynes

Pumpkins

Yummy, scrummy, pumpkin delicious as can be
You should try pumpkin pie, juicy as can be
Lots of pips inside, good to carve at Hallowe'en
Yummiest thing I've ever seen
You should try it, my orange pumpkin.

Hannah Michael (8)
Cold Harbour CE School, Milton Keynes

Travel

I love to travel
It's so much fun
I travel to find the sun.

I went by Sampan to Japan
I went by train to Spain
I went by canoe to Salou.

I love to travel
It's so much fun
I travel to find the sun.

Kathrynn Cook (10)
Cold Harbour CE School, Milton Keynes

Summer

Summer is here
Sizzling and hot
No more rain to fear
Now we can get out a lot.

Beaches full of sand
People in the sea
Lots of travellers on our land
Oh, what a happy time it'll be.

Zoe Zukas (10)
Cold Harbour CE School, Milton Keynes

Leaves

Crunchy,
Crusty,
Delicate,
Colourful,
Rusty leaves
Falling off the trees in the autumn.

Nathan Goodenough (8)
Cold Harbour CE School, Milton Keynes

Summer

When summer comes,
The sun is so bright,
The leaves are green,
And the day is so long and light.

When you look above,
Or play at the park,
You will never stop playing,
Until it gets dark.

I could lie on the grass,
And look up to the sky,
There're so many birds,
And clouds rushing by.

But when summer ends,
We know it was fun,
But autumn has come,
We know there is work to be done.

Gintare Auglyte (10)
Cold Harbour CE School, Milton Keynes

Jack

There once was a man called Jack,
Who had a big red sack,
Every time he dropped the sack
He would get a smack.

Jack lived in a big house,
With only him and his mouse,
People called the mouse Rouse,
He got fed a woodlouse.

Jack lived in a town,
He walked like a clown
And walked about in his dressing gown
Everybody looked and frowned.

Fraser Mackay (10)
Cold Harbour CE School, Milton Keynes

Destiny

Football, football so unpredictable,
You'll never know where the ball is rolling.
Towards the goal, like a bullet, unstoppable,
Let me try another sport a bit like bowling.

Bowling, bowling, is harder than I thought,
You'll never know what it's like to be on the spot.
Maybe then I should try another sport,
And I'll get a try at the million pound jackpot.

Destiny, destiny where will you take me?
Right to the sky or right to Earth.
My dream wish close by a beautiful sea
When I am close by the sea, teach me to surf.

Keep trying, keep trying maybe another time
Fulfil your wishes and your dreams.
I would love some hot tea with lime
I will try again with a successful team.

Rehaan Butt (10)
Cold Harbour CE School, Milton Keynes

Walking In The Forest

Walking in the forest,
Wind blowing through my hair,
Trees swaying in the wind,
Leaves flying in the air.

Walking in the forest,
Squirrels running up the trees,
They are looking all around,
Their fur gently blowing in the breeze.

Walking in the forest,
Seeing the light ahead,
Knowing I'm nearly home,
Looking forward to my bed.

Ellie Sturmey (10)
Cold Harbour CE School, Milton Keynes

My Hamster

I went to the pet shop and spent some dosh,
I bought a hamster and named her Squash.

She is lovely and cute and very sweet,
She stuffs her pouch when she does eat.

She's asleep in the day but at night, she's busy,
On her wheel making herself dizzy.

Her cage is messy but very big,
It's where she burrows and tries to dig.

She is so tiny, not very tall,
She rolls around in her exercise ball.

Her eyes are bright and ruby-red,
She goes to sleep in her warm, cosy bed.

She's the loveliest hamster I ever did get,
I love her so much, she's a brilliant pet.

Lauren Mathieson (10)
Cold Harbour CE School, Milton Keynes

A Unicorn

Unicorns are magical
As you can see
Do you know what they're like?
Well, come and find out with me

This magical creature
Looks like a horse
With a mane just the same
But with powers that take them to the sky

Do you know what is there?
Round the world at night
When you are asleep
Across the land and sea
Do you know what it is?
A unicorn.

Dervla Drinkwater (8)
Cold Harbour CE School, Milton Keynes

Sweet Slow Barbados

Sweet, slow Barbados
So calm and slow,
Quiet and sweet,
So calm and slow.

Sweet, quick Barbados
So quick and fast
Quick and loud
So quick and fast.

Calm, sweet Barbados
So quick and fast,
Time goes so quick
Sweet, slow Barbados
So quick and fast.

Sweet, slow Barbados
So pretty and calm
So romantic and slow
Sweet, slow Barbados.

Rebecca Ruggles (10)
Cold Harbour CE School, Milton Keynes

Cats

Cats are fluffy
Cats are cute
My auntie's cat chewed my boot.
Cats like to eat rats
Cats like to eat bats
Cats like to have their friends over
And like to have little kitty-cat chats.
Cats are very fat
Cats like to curl up on every single mat.

Faye Devonshire (9)
Cold Harbour CE School, Milton Keynes

Friendship

Friendship, friendship
Wonderful friendship
It is a feeling
It is a mood

Friendship, friendship
Great friendship
It is lovable
It is sweet

Friendship, friendship
Lovely friendship
It is the king
It's wicked!

Friendship, friendship
The king, friendship
Worldwide friendship
You are the *best!*

Rosie Barton (10)
Cold Harbour CE School, Milton Keynes

Interesting Facts

What's an interesting fact about you?
I like to play on my PlayStation 2.
What's another interesting fact about you?
I've got lots of games for my PlayStation 2.
What's another interesting fact about you?
I like to play cricket, especially with you.
What's another interesting fact about you?
I like to play football, how about you?

Robert Gerrard (9)
Cold Harbour CE School, Milton Keynes

The Wonders Of The World

I alone shall see the shine of the stars on a winter's night.
I alone shall see the flash of lightning during a summer storm.
I alone shall see the colour of the autumn leaves fall on a dark day.
I alone shall see the flowers come out from their buds on a
spring morning.

All the things around us are colourful and bright
And all we need to do to see them is to open our eyes.

I alone shall see the patterns on a delicate snowflake as it starts
to snow.
I alone shall see the heat of the sun looking down on me.
I alone shall see the brightness of day turn to the darkness of night.
I alone shall see the pleasantness of a newborn baby's very
first smile.

All the things around us are colourful and bright
And all we need to do to see them is to open our eyes.

I alone shall see this brightness
I alone shall see this love
I alone shall see this hard work
I alone shall see this comfort
I alone shall see this happiness
I alone shall see these changes
I alone shall see these colours
I alone shall see these - *wonders!*

Jasmine Brittain (9)
Cold Harbour CE School, Milton Keynes

Conkers

Brown, spiky, whitey, green,
It's really amazing from the conker tree.
The way it cracks right open when it falls.
Shiny, solid, smooth and indestructible.
Sometimes it's really cool the way the horse chestnut breaks with a fall.
Crooked, chocolaty, cracking, spotty,
Breaks, it falls and that is all.

Tunde Awojobi (9)
Cold Harbour CE School, Milton Keynes

What Astronauts Do In Space

Astronauts glide really high
Having fun in the sky;
Scientists think they're on a mission
But actually they're alien fishin'

The astronauts are playing football in space
One of them got hit in the face;
But it didn't hit him very hard
Because of the gravity on planet Mars.

Astronauts try to sleep at night
But they're next to the sun so it's way too bright;
They put on their pyjamas and go to bed
They're dreaming of Martians in their head.

Astronauts fly their rocket really fast
In a race it will never come last;
10,9,8,7,6,5,4,3,2,1
They play with strange stuff while they head towards the sun.

That's what astronauts do in space.

Danial Naqvi (9)
Cold Harbour CE School, Milton Keynes

Balloons

Balloons fly like birds, they fly in the sky
To different countries.
They interest people so much,
They do tricks in the sky,
They have big heads which can see everything,
They like to eat worms and caterpillars,
Balloons get killed by big birds.

Jason Acquaah (10)
Cold Harbour CE School, Milton Keynes

But

I thought I could get away with it
I really, really thought so,
But I have a teacher
Who would always check my homework.
I thought I could miss detention
I really, really thought so,
But I have a teacher
Who would always keep her eyes on me.
I thought the headteacher wouldn't care
I really, really thought so,
But I have a teacher
Who always makes sure I get there.
I thought my teacher was just joking
I really, really thought so,
But I have a teacher
Who just went and phoned my mum.
I thought I could have forgotten it
I really, really thought so,
But I have a mum
Who just grounded me.

Jessica Tsoi (11)
Cold Harbour CE School, Milton Keynes

My Bro

My brother, my bro
Is he helpful? Oh no!
He eats a lot and talks
He barely ever walks
He just sits and slouches on the couches,
His bible is the Argos catalogue and he reads it all day
But I would miss him if he was gone, all the same.

Yasmine Taherbeigi (10)
Cold Harbour CE School, Milton Keynes

My Favourite Things

My favourite lesson is literacy
My teacher is hilarious
She makes the lesson so exciting
And she makes me so happy
I want to come the next day.

My favourite thing, my favourite thing
Is literacy in the morning.

My favourite day is Christmas
They give me lots of gifts
And I like to see my old relatives
Faces grinning with wrinkly skin and joy.

My favourite day, my favourite day
Is the happy business of Christmas.

James Cloke (9)
Cold Harbour CE School, Milton Keynes

Conkers

I am very bumpy, hard as a nut
I am sometimes tough, very round like a sphere
Look really tasty, like chocolate
Have a white bit at the top
I am rock solid.

Ryan Johnston (7)
Cold Harbour CE School, Milton Keynes

My Room

My room is full of toys
No girls allowed in, only boys
I sleep there every night
My bed is warm, it's just right.

Harry Kennedy (8)
Cold Harbour CE School, Milton Keynes

Summary

S unshine so bright, too hot to sleep at night.
U nder the sun where the people are playing, splashing in pools
and having some fun.
M ums all around are trying to keep cool, children at play
are acting like fools.
M essing around, school holidays begun, playing with friends
and my mum.
E xciting days out at theme parks and zoos, a lot of people
using the loos.
R unning around and eating lunch, stopping our bike ride
to have a quick munch.

Bethany Hunt (8)
Cold Harbour CE School, Milton Keynes

Chelsea

C helsea are cool.
H ooray! We are the best.
E veryone loves Chelsea.
L ondon based.
S tamford Bridge, the place they play.
E veryone loves Chelsea.
A way, away we're off to watch them play.

Josh Rodger (7)
Cold Harbour CE School, Milton Keynes

Leaves

L eaves are all different shapes.
E lms have rough-edged leaves.
A holly's leaves has sharp edges.
V ariety of different leaves.
E lder leaves are zigzagged.
S tone pine has needled leaves.

Adam Goyen (7)
Cold Harbour CE School, Milton Keynes

Summer

Superbikes

S uzuki is a very fast bike and I mean it.
U nbelievably huge exhausts that make the bikes go up to 210mph.
P retty mopeds chugging along.
E very motorbike is nice.
R iding a motorbike takes skill.
B ogey is my uncle Steve's nickname because he wears green
                                                            leathers.
I think my uncle is mad on his motorbike.
K ids should never ride on the back of bikes.
E very rider should be responsible on the road and wear the
                                                            proper kit.
S uperbikes are quick, so be careful.

James Honhold (9)
Cold Harbour CE School, Milton Keynes

Dinner Plates

D inner, dinner, good to eat,
I n dinner we don't eat wheat,
N ever in my life am I going to have Tic Tacs,
N ever in my life am I going to eat Blu-tack,
E very day I have dinner,
R ound the table to have some food.

P lates to eat off,
L ucky to have food in the house,
A te a piece of ham,
T ea, dinner at the same time,
E veryone is nice and good,
S melling food makes you want to eat.

Jonathan House (9)
Cold Harbour CE School, Milton Keynes

The Start Of Spring

In the morning
The sun shines in the sky
While the clouds pass by
The birds sing
Flying with their wings.

In the afternoon
I eat my lunch
And go outside
To pick flowers by the bunch
I play with joy
With some toys.

At night
I get changed
I have my dinner
My books arranged
Homework done
I go to bed with lots of fun!

Mamie-Kate Naughton-Ammon (8)
Cold Harbour CE School, Milton Keynes

The Great Day

I was playing football
It was a great day.
I was playing tag
It was a great day.
I was talking to my friends
It was a great day.
I got full marks
It was a great day.
I had a great lunch
It was a great day.
It was a sunny day
It was a great day.
I scored a goal in football
It was a great day!

Ryan Smith (9)
Cold Harbour CE School, Milton Keynes

Food

Food is yummy,
Food is great,
Food is good,
To share with your mate.

Pizza is saucy,
Pizza is cool,
Pizza is more tasty,
Than anything at all.

Apples are crunchy,
Apples are sweet,
Apples are juicy
And apples are good for me.

Pasta is smooth,
Pasta is curly,
Pasta is usually
Very swirly.

Grapes are delicious,
Grapes are nice,
Grapes can be green,
Or they can be white.

Soup can be thick,
Soup can be runny,
On cold winter days,
It warms up my tummy.

Raspberries are sour,
Raspberries are sweet,
Raspberries are very
Nice to eat.

Chocolate is brown,
Chocolate is white,
Chocolate is one of
My favourite delights.

Hana Robson (9)
Cold Harbour CE School, Milton Keynes

Planet Dream

Planet Dream is a sacred place,
Where the good dreams come true!
Just one little dream and you zoom away
Travelling to the central star.

You can climb the tallest mountain,
Swim in the deepest ocean,
Fly in the highest sky,
Relax under the hottest sun!

Only a true dreamer comes here,
For this is a planet of dreams.
What you dream is up to you,
Remember, good dreams come true.

The laughter of children
Keeps the whole planet peaceful,
The loving and caring people
Make the planet beautiful!

The sun never goes away,
It shines night and day.
The sky is the purest blue,
Oh look! A rainbow just for you!

Karrie Adams (10)
Cold Harbour CE School, Milton Keynes

Cakes

Big cakes, little cakes, middle-sized cakes,
All sorts of shaped cakes!
One cake, two cakes, three cakes, four cakes
How many cakes are there?
Blue cakes, red cakes, yellow cakes, green cakes
All sorts of coloured cakes!

Freya Berry (7)
Cold Harbour CE School, Milton Keynes

The Summer Holiday

Hooray, hooray, it's the summer holiday.
We are off school,
For six weeks,
It will be very cool!

No more early mornings,
No more school,
No more homework,
Just football!

It will be very good,
After we set off for our holiday,
I am so excited,
I just have to wait!

No more reading,
The only time you're allowed to talk,
Now it's the summer holidays,
We can talk, talk, talk!

Yippee,
Hooray, hooray, it's the summer holiday!

Jonathan Osae (9)
Cold Harbour CE School, Milton Keynes

The Day I Sank Through The Drain

The day I sank through the drain
Was a very peculiar day
I was cleaning my teeth when I tripped
And fell in the bath
I started to shrink!
Then my sister started a bath
When she pulled the plug I started to scream
As I was sucked down the sticky drain
I felt a shake, I was awake
In my bed.

Sam Ward (9)
Cold Harbour CE School, Milton Keynes

Babies

Babies, babies, babies all around us,
Why, oh why do they make such a fuss?
Change their nappies,
Clean their beds,
They make you go all pink and red.
Hot and flustered, hot and flustered.
Babies, babies, babies all around us,
Why, oh why do they make such a fuss?
Feed them bottles,
Hold their heads,
They make lots of noise when they want to be fed.
Hungry and grumbly, hungry and grumbly.
Babies, babies, babies all around us,
Why, oh why do they make such a fuss?
Give them Calpol,
Share our love,
Listen to Mummy cooing like a dove.
Cold and shivery, cold and shivery.
Babies, babies, babies all around us,
Why, oh why do they make such a fuss?
Push their prams,
Shake their toys,
They like to stare at girls and boys.
Giggles and laughs, giggles and laughs.

Hannah Berry (9)
Cold Harbour CE School, Milton Keynes

On My Own

On my own a see-saw will always be down
On my own I can't play Pictionary
On my own I can't play football
On my own I can't send letters to someone
On my own I can't email anyone
On my own I can't do the posh dance or waltz.

Gemma White (9)
Cold Harbour CE School, Milton Keynes

The Meaning Of Life Is A Tree

The meaning of life is a tree
And soon you'll be able to see,
Now read on carefully.

We all start off as a seed,
Merely the size of a bead,
And as the years go by,
Our weakness starts to die.

Then you get stronger,
Taller and wider too,
Like the thickening branches of a tree,
That is what they do.

I hope that explains it clearly,
Now that you can see,
That the meaning of life is simply,
An ordinary tree.

Ryan Rumsey (9)
Cold Harbour CE School, Milton Keynes

Holiday Blues

I just got back from holiday, had a really good time,
The room was really nice and we got a free bottle of wine.

Woke up in the morning, the sun was very bright,
Still felt groggy after a very long flight.

Couldn't wait to go outside and jump into the pool,
The water was very clear, refreshing and cool.

I made a new friend and Natasha was her name,
We spent most days in the pool playing fun games.

Even though the food wasn't great, I'd love to go there again,
While we were in Turkey there was no wind or rain.

We arrived home on Tuesday, nothing much had changed,
Can't wait for Mum and Dad to take me on holiday again.

Melissa Jones (9)
Cold Harbour CE School, Milton Keynes

My Family And Friends

My mum is Karren,
My dad is Darren,
I am Daisy and I am totally crazy!
My little sis makes my life bliss,
Although she can be a little miss!
I love my family, yes I do,
I love going to Brownies and I love beef stew.
Me and my friends have lots of fun,
In the playground we like to run.
Skipping, laughing and talking too,
When it is wet play,
We play 'Guess Who?'
I love to visit my nan's on a Sunday,
With my cousin Nicole there, it becomes a fun day.
Nan cooks dinner,
While we play,
Grandad goes fishing all day!
My dog's called Kane,
Sometimes he can be a pain.
I hate toys,
I hate boys,
I like making noise.
My favourite colour is pink,
Me and Darcy are a perfect link.
I go to Cold Harbour school
And I think it's really cool.
Our school jumpers are red,
Eight o'clock is when I go to bed.
I always try different trends,
I love my family, I like my friends.

Daisy Lynch (9)
Cold Harbour CE School, Milton Keynes

My Family

This is a poem about my family.
We will start with me cos I am Emily.

I was the youngest
But then came a brother
We also have Dave
Who's in love with my mother

Then there is Katie
She is my matey
She is four years older
And very much bolder

Next sister is Hannah
She played the piana
She's now into soccer
Let's hope she don't come a cropper

Next is big sis Leanne
She is seventeen
Mostly she is really nice
But when she is tired, she can be mean

And last but not least
There is my brother Jack
He gurgles and giggles
When lying on his back

So he is now the baby
It is no longer me
But all I have to say right now is
I love my family!

Emily Stapleton (9)
Cold Harbour CE School, Milton Keynes

The Day My Cat Ate A Frog

C andy, my cat, is a bit stupid
A nd he likes to eat a lot of food too
T oday he did something quite yucky

A nd ate a full size frog, *yew!*
T omorrow he has to eat cat food
E ven I think that is true

F ranny next door was crying
R obert was the frog's name too
O ggy is the name of Franny's other frog
G ranny came at the end of the day with her dog.

Lydia Mahon (9)
Cold Harbour CE School, Milton Keynes

My Poem

B irthdays - a day to be happy and enjoy being older
I t's a time to celebrate
R eally fun
T ime to open presents
H ats and party bags add fun
D ads and mums giving presents
A fter presents, birthday cakes
Y esterday young, today older.

Lewis Burt (10)
Cold Harbour CE School, Milton Keynes

Disney

D riving around everywhere trying to go on all of the rides.
I nteresting sights to see everywhere you look.
S eeing all the characters and getting their autographs.
N o one is unhappy because they're at Disneyland.
E veryone is there, they go to all of the shows at the end of the day.
Y ou would love to be there and I already have been!

David Orange (9)
Cold Harbour CE School, Milton Keynes

My Rabbit

My favourite pet is my bunny
He's white and fluffy with a big tummy.

Sniffles never answers to his name
But really he is very tame.

He loves to be put out in his run
Especially in the midday sun.

He hops and skips all around
Then he just lies on the ground.

Sometimes he likes to dig a big hole
Anyone would think he was a mole

When it comes to his food
He sometimes gets in a mood

He throws his bowl upside down
And looks as though he has a frown.

He stamps his feet to let me know
How angry he is if I go.

He makes a nest in his hay
Which I have to clean every day.

I like to stroke behind his ears
He would let me do it for years and years.

Before long he closes his eyes
Then I creep away saying my goodbyes.

Charlotte Ring (9)
Cold Harbour CE School, Milton Keynes

The Pig

My wonderful pig lives in a sty
I think he has always wanted to fly
I see him watch the birds go by
All he does is sit and cry
And that's why I think he wants to try.

Wesley Sherratt (10)
Cold Harbour CE School, Milton Keynes

Dave

My dog's name is Dave
He is never well behaved
He barks at guests
And eats my vests
But he is the best.

Dad walks him at night
Because he can see without the light
If you met him he would give you a fright
But he is the best.

He loves his cuddles
And likes playing in puddles
He's always in trouble
But he is the best.

Taylor Stewart (10)
Cold Harbour CE School, Milton Keynes

Summer Times

I love summer with a soft, hot breeze,
The dandelions that make you sneeze!
No one with an angry frown,
Just happy smiles all around.

How about a picnic in the sun?
With a bite into a hot, sticky bun.
Jump into the swimming pool,
Gosh, it's brilliantly cool.

I love summer with a soft, hot breeze,
The dandelions that make you sneeze!
No one with an angry frown,
Just happy smiles all around.

Aimée Lewington (10)
Cold Harbour CE School, Milton Keynes

The Chase Is On

His legs start to move
Ignition kicks in
Blood runs through his veins
Petrol pumps through the pipes
His legs start to move,
The wheels start to roll
The chase is on!
Prey in jaws
Flags been waved
His heart goes slow
Engine goes silent.

Chris Showler (10)
Cold Harbour CE School, Milton Keynes

My Family

Loving mum, caring dad,
There for me, even if I'm bad.
Playful brother, two cute cats,
One great dog and magic grandads.

Lots of cousins, aunties too,
Many uncles and a nanny (one too few).
Altogether a great family,
That's all of them and little ol' me.

Zoe Morris (9)
Cold Harbour CE School, Milton Keynes

The Dragon

The dragon is the sky
He sweeps across the land like a bullet
He sulks when the rain drops
Then he sweeps across the land
To his dark, scary cave.

Jake Tighe (10)
Cold Harbour CE School, Milton Keynes

What Makes Me Happy . . .

Is my brother wearing make-up as army camouflage
Is being tickled on the feet
Is eating jam roly-poly till I'm full
Is watching my cousin swear and cry at the same time
Is seeing my friend jump off the garage onto the trampoline
Is playing on the PlayStation
Is having a daydream of whatever I want
Is chewing my dad's sock
Is going to the loo for a poo
Is looking at my happy list when I'm in a bad mood.

Sam Jordan (9)
Cold Harbour CE School, Milton Keynes

What Makes Me Sad

What makes me sad . . .
Is people picking on my friends
Is getting out of my warm, cosy bed and getting hurt
Is getting told off when I didn't do anything
Is having someone say something about my grandad,
                                        because he's dead
Is when my dad has a fight with my mum
Is when I'm sick!

Yaw Ofosu (9)
Cold Harbour CE School, Milton Keynes

What Am I?

I am a shiny diamond flashing from the clouds.
I am zigzagging flashes of smashed glass stretching across the sky.
I am long spikes of white streaks below Heaven.
I am shiny icicles flowing through the air.
I am lightning.

Ben Percy (9)
Denfield Park Junior School, Rushden

What Am I?

I am a fluffy cloud, mesmerizing children as I float down.
I am a puffy marshmallow carried to the top of a snowman.
I am smooth cream, stirred round by little feet.
I am soft cotton wool, *so* inviting to touch.
I am a silky blanket, flowing onto the ground.
I am a dream-like feather, sweeping down to Earth.
I am a piece of Heaven, nestling into a hole of boredom.

A: I am snow.

Elenore Linsell (9)
Denfield Park Junior School, Rushden

What Am I?

I am pale, feathery pillows drifting around the Earth.
I am white, puffy candyfloss floating through the air.
I am fluffy cotton wool below the sparkling sun.
I am a layer of snow covering the sky.
I am silky marshmallows following the wind.
I am sheep in the sky, grazing in the air.
I am a layer of tasty icing taking over from the blue.
I am clouds.

Jodie Pitfield (9)
Denfield Park Junior School, Rushden

What Am I?

I am a soft, white duvet that lays across cornfields.
I am a slippery silk sheet covering the road.
I am sharp daggers covering the road.
I am smooth paper spreading over the land.
I am white velvet covering the cave.
What am I?

I am ice.

Emily McAlwane (9)
Denfield Park Junior School, Rushden

What Am I?

I am white, ice-cold snowflakes flickering through the sky.
I am big, round, colourful marbles falling onto the ground.
I am bright diamonds crashing onto the earth.
I am bright white cotton wool pouring onto the window sill.
I am trickling tears of sadness falling from the sky.
I am rainbow-coloured petals floating to the path.
I am yellow sweetcorn tumbling onto the cars.
I am purple-coloured berries splattering into the garden.
I am sweet, ripe strawberries falling behind the hill.
I am small, round peas tumbling off the roof.
I am juicy, green pears splashing onto the lake.
I am rain.

Sasha Harris (9)
Denfield Park Junior School, Rushden

The Train

Clickety-clack, clickety-clack,
The train is speeding down the track.
Clickety-clock, clickety-clock,
Will we get there at twelve o'clock?
We are going through a tunnel,
Steam is coming from our funnel.
I am going to see my mate,
I hope I will not be late.
Slowing, slowing, slowing, coming to a halt,
We are a bit late, but it's not my fault.
The station's near,
I see a deer.
It's crossing the track.
Screech!
We have stopped,
But it's three o'clock.

Max Rolfe (9)
Gayhurst School, Gerrards Cross

Train Poem

Slamming doors, people asleep,
The wheels go round but no one peeps.

Screeching wheels, people shout all around,
The train moving off, we're going underground.

Steam from the train, whistle goes,
Shouting to the train driver and off we go!

Rumble, rumble, round and round,
Never to stop that terrible sound.

Never to stop, never ever,
Through the wind and snowy weather.

Coming up hills, going down through,
Manchester, Chelsea and Liverpool town.

Round and round to a stop, slowing with a jerk of shock,
We're on time according to the clock.

Alex Mann (9)
Gayhurst School, Gerrards Cross

The Train

Slowly, slowly, the train starts slowly,
Clickety-clack, clickety-clack,
the train goes faster down the track,
Through a field and in a tunnel,
into a station like a funnel,
Speeding, zooming, thundering past,
Just how long will this big blur last?
Slowing down to a halt,
Some are late, but it's not our fault.

Matthew O'Regan (10)
Gayhurst School, Gerrards Cross

Limericks

One day at the seaside I saw,
A rather large, pink dinosaur.
It gave me a wave,
Then ran in a cave,
And came out with my father-in-law.

I was walking one day in a wood,
When I talked to a friend, Robin Hood.
He gave me a bow
And also said, 'Hello,'
And he ran off to get up to no good.

Sitting one day under a tree,
You'll never guess who I happened to see.
Why, it was Frank Lampard,
Wearing a pink leotard,
While he sang a loud jamboree.

Skipping a rope is what I play,
When I do ten, I shout, 'Hooray.'
All of my friends,
Cheers they send,
When I skip in the month of May.

Rockets that soar, cars that drive,
Bees that make honey in their hives.
So much to do,
But I haven't a clue,
Why we sleep for most of our lives.

Amit Patel (11)
Gayhurst School, Gerrards Cross

Winter

Freezing, beautiful
Snowing, shivering, aching
Always a chilling sensation
Season.

Max Johnston (10)
Gayhurst School, Gerrards Cross

Mother Duck Rap

There was an old woman, Mother Duck,
Who always thought like a hockey puck.
She went to a game,
Which was really lame,
Boy, was she out of her luck!

Mother Duck was such a quack,
That she broke her crooked back.
At the GP,
She was full of glee,
A soccer team made her centre back.

Her husband is called Father Goose,
He looks like a rather big moose.
He likes to eat orange peel
And likes electric eel,
But this is of very little use.

Father Goose is so overweight,
He can't fit through his own front gate.
Because he can't fit through any doors,
He sometimes breaks his own special laws,
By always being very late!

Mother Duck thinks she's really cool
And always thinks she supremely rules.
'I'm queen of the world,'
She says with a twirl,
When all she does is drool.

Parus Nischal (10)
Gayhurst School, Gerrards Cross

New York

Amazing, paradise,
Huge, yellow, wild,
The amazing Big Apple
Quality.

Christopher Katanchian (10)
Gayhurst School, Gerrards Cross

Limericks

There was a cat called Mo,
Who had a brother called Jo.
One day in a bar,
They saw their grandma,
Who sent them to Monaco.

There once lived a man from Kent,
Who travelled by bus to Trent.
One day on the road,
He saw a fat toad
So the bus headed back to Gent.

There once was a camel from Mars,
Who would eat nothing but chocolate bars.
One day in a shop,
The shopkeeper said, 'Stop!
Or I'll put all your chocolates in jars.'

There once was a woman called Jill,
Who sat on a window sill.
One windy day,
On her sill she did sway
And fell and herself she did kill.

There once was a rat called Dave,
Who surfed on a massive wave.
The wave was too high,
He flew into the sky
And landed near the mouth of a cave.

Toby Foster (10)
Gayhurst School, Gerrards Cross

Biscuits

Biscuits,
Crunchy, tasty,
Sitting, waiting, leaning,
Always there to crunch,
Food!

Sam Zatland (10)
Gayhurst School, Gerrards Cross

Limericks

There was an old man called Simo
He owned a very long limo
He was driving one day
But got locked away
For running over a hippo.

There once was a genius from Esser
Whose knowledge grew lesser and lesser
At last it grew so small
He knew nothing at all
And now he is a college professor.

There once was a lady named Bright
Whose speed was much faster than light
She set out one day
In a very flashy way
And returned on the previous night.

There once was a lady from France
Who decided to take a chance
So she bet every pound
On a skinny greyhound
And now she's suffering a trance.

There once was a man from Great Britain
Who interrupted two girls knitting
He said with a sigh
'That park bench, well I
Painted it right where you're sitting.'

Harrypal Panesar (10)
Gayhurst School, Gerrards Cross

The Frog - Haiku

The very small frog,
Leaping across the river,
Its tongue catching flies.

Jack Baker (10)
Gayhurst School, Gerrards Cross

The Race

Thud! Thud! Thud! Is the heart of an athlete before he starts a
tiring race.
Run! Run! Run! Is the scream of a fan cheering as the runners
begin the chase.
Quickly! Quickly! Quickly! Is the speed of the runners when they
start the long, hard race.
Faster! Faster! Faster! Is the cheer of a fan when the athletes
pick up the pace.
Boom! Boom! Boom! is the shoe of an athlete when it hits the
running track.
C'mon! C'mon! C'mon! is the shout of a supporter when their
favourite falls to the back.
Gasp! Gasp! Gasp! Is the noise of the winner catching his breath
at the end of the race.
Yes! Yes! Yes! Is the voice of his wife gazing dreamily into his face.

Adam Jackson (9)
Gayhurst School, Gerrards Cross

The Vampire Snake

Something slithering through the clear moonlight,
Blood so hot and warmed,
The vampire snake,
King of the afterlife,
Sinister, mighty, invincible,
Like a ghoul haunting Windsor Castle,
Like Jack the Ripper in snake form,
It makes me feel scared,
Like the tsunami covering the whole of the Thai coast,
The vampire snake,
Reminds you of the torture prisons in Hell.

Ryan Campkin (10)
Gayhurst School, Gerrards Cross

My Friend In The Night

The night is dark and gloomy,
The howling wind has woken me.
Twigs and leaves rustle,
I look out of my bedroom window,
I think I can see shadows moving,
But it is only the wind,
Blowing at the bushes.
They move from side to side,
Suddenly they hear a howl,
I hear a creak,
I hear soft, running footsteps,
Coming towards my bedroom door.
My door slowly opens,
I shiver in my slippers,
But it is only my dog, Blaze,
He runs up to me and licks my face.

Christopher Neophytou (9)
Gayhurst School, Gerrards Cross

The Chase

There was a small spider,
Who met a big tiger,
Out in the jungle one day.
The tiger wanted to eat the small spider,
So the spider crawled away.

But then the big tiger,
Caught sight of the spider,
As he hurried away.
The spider thought fast
And spun a web,
Bigger than the tiger's head,
Catching the tiger until was *dead*.

Bradley Stone (9)
Gayhurst School, Gerrards Cross

Vampire Poem

From the coffin a vampire appears,
Fangs covered in blood with pointy ears,
The bat-like cape, those blood-red eyes,
Causes death, shrieks and cries.
He sucks up blood from our race,
A look of hate upon his face,
So if you ever see one,
You can stop looking, just run!

Robert Sutherland (9)
Gayhurst School, Gerrards Cross

Grapes

Grapes
The fruit of the gods
Oval, green, juicy
As oval as a rugby ball
As juicy as exotic fruits
It makes me feel huge
Like a giant in front of small humans
Grapes
Remind us how lucky we are to be living.

Hugo Davis (10)
Gayhurst School, Gerrards Cross

Stage Fright

I practised all day,
I practised all night,
But I was afraid I'd get stage fright.
Then the night came,
When I went on stage,
I got out my instrument
And *oh!* what great music I played.
However, I was still afraid I'd get stage fright.

Daniel Steele (10)
Gayhurst School, Gerrards Cross

The Amazing Sea

The amazing sea
The water and foam glide together
Like a huge piece of watery land
Sweet, relaxed and pure
Like a blue, horizontal skyscraper
It makes me feel tiny
Like a small ant that nobody notices
The amazing sea
Reminds me of how big the world is.

Samuel Millard (10)
Gayhurst School, Gerrards Cross

The Championship

The big football tournament
Is on only once a year
This year it's in Kent
And the winner gets a big bottle of beer
Most of the countries are there
But some dropped out in the qualifying round
Some teams don't care
A few dropped out without a sound.

Julian Knoester (10)
Gayhurst School, Gerrards Cross

The Rainbow

Red, like the blood of the innocent
Orange, like the glow of flames
Yellow, an image of the sun
Green, the colour of my eyes
Blue, the waters of Heaven
Indigo, the colour of grapes
Violet, some lovely flowers.

Bertie Martine (10)
Gayhurst School, Gerrards Cross

Eagle

Medium,
Very feathery,
Diving down,
All eagle,
Gliding wings,
Ferocious,
Dangerous,
Like an aeroplane,
Oh eagle,
Deadly to birds,
Oh eagle,
Oh eagle.

George Lawley (8)
Gayhurst School, Gerrards Cross

My Tiger

Fierce,
Massive,
Strong,
Tiger,
Running fast to the jungle,
Powerful,
Terrifying,
It can move like a motorbike,
I like you, elegant tiger,
Fierce tiger.

Joshua Kirby (8)
Gayhurst School, Gerrards Cross

The Tiger

Big and strong,
Fierce,
Legs move very quickly,
Moves dangerously and fast,
Moves strongly,
Fierce as a lion,
Colourful stripes,
I like the way it moves,
Tiger, tiger!
Fierce,
Tiger, tiger!
Roar!

Matthew Pugh (9)
Gayhurst School, Gerrards Cross

Lion

Fierce
Agile
King of the jungle
Lion
It moves as fast as a superbike
Pouncing on animals
Scares others away
I like you, colourful lion
Lion, lion
Ferocious lion.

Alex Deninson (8)
Gayhurst School, Gerrards Cross

The Hedgehog

He needs:
A spiky coat like thorns,
A tiny head like an apple,
Big, wide eyes like a full moon,
Tiny paws, as tiny as a rock.
He can:
Roll up into a ball like a football,
Hide himself in thorns.
He eats:
Snails,
Slugs,
Worms,
Eggs,
Cockroaches.

Conor Arnot (8)
Gayhurst School, Gerrards Cross

The Westie Rap

I'm the Westie from the west.
I may be a pestie,
But I'm a Westie.
I shoot like a cowboy,
But I don't shoot cows.
So praise to the west,
Not the east,
Or the north,
Not even the south.
Because I'm Westie
And I'm here to please.

Charlie West (10)
Gayhurst School, Gerrards Cross

The Fox

Fast
Orange
Soft
Fox
Running
Like the
Wind
Quickly
Sneakily
As orange as a pumpkin
I don't know what I would
Do without
Fox
Soft fox.

Brodie Steele (9)
Gayhurst School, Gerrards Cross

The Tiger

Very ferocious
And absolutely camouflaged,
A killer of meat,
Tiger,
It moves swiftly through the grass,
Brilliantly fast when catching prey,
It is like a plane at top speed!
I will be frightened by its teeth,
Which are as white as white.
Tiger,
Meat-eating tiger.

Ross Buckley (8)
Gayhurst School, Gerrards Cross

The Cat

Furry and cute
Mini
Soft
The cat.
He uses his legs to walk slowly,
The cat is quiet,
He lives on land,
He likes to nap.
He feels very furry and soft,
The cat,
Shy cat.
Miaow!

Oliver Levi (8)
Gayhurst School, Gerrards Cross

Lion

Fast,
Killer,
Fierce,
Lion.
It moves like a car,
It moves like the smooth wind,
It attacks like a shark.
I like the way it runs
Lion,
Fast lion.

Andile Mathebula (8)
Gayhurst School, Gerrards Cross

The Roaring Lion

Fierce
Roaring
Yellow
The lion
Raging through the forest
Furiously
Angrily
As deadly as a great white shark
I would be the loneliest thing on Earth
Without it
The lion
Fierce lion.

Siddharth Saraogi (8)
Gayhurst School, Gerrards Cross

Monkey

Swinging
Funny
Mischief
Monkey
Jumping from tree to tree
Lively
Quick
As brown as chocolate
I would be unhappy without you
Monkey
Funny monkey.

Charles Galligan (9)
Gayhurst School, Gerrards Cross

The Scary Slide

There was a slide,
In my garden,
It was so high
I started to cry,
My mum came out,
So I started to shout,
I was forced
To slide of course,
I went down the slide
Like a king with pride,
I landed on the dirt,
It really started to hurt,
I will never do it again!

Connor Broadley (10)
Gayhurst School, Gerrards Cross

A Mouse

Tiny,
Furry,
Has a tail,
Mouse.
Fast, sly and quick,
Soft and swift,
It moves as fast as a person.
Mouse, I like your fur,
Oh lovely mouse.

Oliver Phipps (8)
Gayhurst School, Gerrards Cross

Horse

Large
Squashy
Lovely
Horse
Jumps up speedily
Elevated
Willing
Orange as a sunflower
I would be gloomy if you went away
Horse
Lovely horse.

Cameron Conn (8)
Gayhurst School, Gerrards Cross

Crocodile

Deadly
Sharp
Cruel
Crocodile
Kills its prey with a lash of its tail
Slowly
Powerfully
Fast
I would feel unhappy without it
Crocodile!

Joshua Ferguson (8)
Gayhurst School, Gerrards Cross

The Spider

There is a spider on the wall,
What should I do?
Tell my mum,
Or whack it with a shoe?

Wait a minute,
It's running away.
Is it going to spin a web
Or maybe going to play?

That cheeky spider's got a smile on its face,
I think it's going to hide in Dad's briefcase.
Oh no it's not, it's heading for the drain,
I must save it before it is never seen again.

Jack Butler (9)
Gayhurst School, Gerrards Cross

The Woods At Night

Blustery wind rustles the leaves,
Sly foxes are out hunting,
Owls pick up mice,
Squirrels seek for nuts,
Animals are safe from hunters,
Leaves on the ground skip around,
Birds are not heard,
Wolves howl viciously,
Bats will flutter quickly,
Who said the woods were not busy at night!

Elliot Van Barthold (9)
Gayhurst School, Gerrards Cross

The Vampire Poem

The bloodsucking vampire, creeping past corners,
No one finds out, as he leaps past them.
If anyone sees, he sucks their blood
With his sharp, evil, bloody teeth.
'There's no such thing as vampires,' I say to myself,
But the dim light is as red as *blood*.

Now the vampire reaches our house,
Sucking people's blood on the way.
He tricks the door lock with his sharp, mighty fingers
And slithers like a worm past the kitchen
And into my room . . .
Argh!

Aarib Khan (9)
Gayhurst School, Gerrards Cross

Sea

As the waves crash and bash against the shore,
Underwater, a shark snaps its jaw.
There is another world in the sea,
Sometimes not seen.
The sea is like a blue duvet,
It covers animals and the Earth.
The sea makes you feel calm
And also quite scared.
Sea creatures have a hard life,
Having to be aware of predators.
The sea is like a stuck record,
Always splash, splash against the shore.

William Bowen (9)
Gayhurst School, Gerrards Cross

Winter

Winter crept
Through the whispering wood
Hushing fir and oak;
Cracked each leaf and froze every web -
But never a word he spoke.

Winter prowled
By the shivering sea,
Lifting sand and stone;
Nipped each nymphet silently -
And then moved on.

Winter raced
Down the frozen stream,
Catching his breath;
On his lips were icicles -
At his back was death.

George Nolan (10)
Gayhurst School, Gerrards Cross

Shark

Deadly
Huge
Dumb
Shark
Stalking its prey
Powerfully
Moves as fast as light
I would feel unhappy if it died
Shark.

Joseph Bull (8)
Gayhurst School, Gerrards Cross

Cars

I like cars, all kinds of cars.
I like fast cars,
Like the Pagani Zonda,
To the NSX Honda.

I like cars, all kinds of cars,
I like posh cars,
Like the Volkswagen Phaeton,
To the Rolls-Royce Phantom.

I like cars, all kinds of cars,
I like classy cars,
Like the Cadillac CTS,
To the Lexus GS.
I like cars.

Sean Gray (9)
Gayhurst School, Gerrards Cross

Ape

Dumb
Scary
Mean
Ape
Swinging from tree to tree
Fast
Amazing
Smelly as burnt toast
I would be lonely without you, ape
Scary ape.

Kayal Patel (7)
Gayhurst School, Gerrards Cross

Food

Food is delicious, there's not enough to load
I want to eat food until my tummy explodes
Some foods are *nice*, like sweets and meat
But all the vegetables in the world, I will *never eat*
But eating lots of fat can make you very ill
So I will eat my vegetables, *I will, I will*
But I won't cut down on sweets and fat
Oh no, no, no, I won't do that!

Barnaby Wilson (10)
Gayhurst School, Gerrards Cross

Football

The glee I had when I scored the winning goal,
It felt like I was king of the world.
It was the best time of my life,
The cheering I heard as I ran around the stadium.
My team members came running up to me,
With beams on their faces.
What a great sensation I had,
We'd won by a goal.

Callum James (9)
Gayhurst School, Gerrards Cross

Rock Star Chicken

R ock star chicken
O utside the door
C atching evil
K ids are fans of rock

S limy walls
T rash on the floor
A nts in the fridge
R ubbish on the roof.

Timothy Hatton (9)
Gayhurst School, Gerrards Cross

Football

F ast is what you need to be to play the game
O wn goals are what you shouldn't be scoring
O ranges are what you get at half-time in schools
T ough and aggressive you need to be to get the ball
B alls made out of pigs' bladders are what they first used
A ll is everything, everything is all . . . you need to get the ball
L etting the opposition get the ball is all you need to do to be a fool
L astly, no dangerous tackles or the way you're going is straight
to the tunnel.

Harish Malhi (10)
Gayhurst School, Gerrards Cross

Rock Star Chicken

R ock star chicken loves to rock
O n his door it says 'Please, please knock'
C ake is his favourite food
K icking puts him in a really good mood

S creaming he hears every day
T error does not get in his way
A mazing sights he does see
R iding his rock rocket is as good as can be.

Thomas Mockridge (9)
Gayhurst School, Gerrards Cross

Rabbit

R abbit racing around the rooms
A nd hopping up and down madly in the green grass
B ecause he is too cute for words, I love to stroke him
B ut he is quick to bite when you touch his delicious foods
I f you're lucky enough, you will get a lick
T he best thing of all is when his fluffy, brown ears stick up!

Seyvan Kellay (9)
Gayhurst School, Gerrards Cross

Limerick

There once was a great big ruler,
That was very peculiar,
Because it couldn't rule a straight line,
But the owner loved to dine,
Her name was Julia and she was way cooler.

There once was a man from Senegal,
Who was brilliant at football.
He scored goals
And played bowls,
But loved to do flips in the hall.

There was a boy called Bill,
Who didn't have lungs but a gill.
He stayed in some water,
Where he saw a dog and bought 'er,
Then leapt on the window sill.

A young boy had to take an exam,
But his car ran over a lamb.
He got out to see,
Then went for a wee
And home for some ham.

There once was a girl from Trent,
Whose bike was ever so bent.
She got it fixed,
Met a boy and kissed,
Then hired a car for rent.

Chris Hayes (10)
Gayhurst School, Gerrards Cross

The Lonely Tree

The weeping willow tree,
The lonely one in the park,
It stood there on its own,
With only the birds and stream to see.
This was the lonely tree.
It wept over the river like a weeping lady,
With its leaves flowing in the stream.
This was the lonely tree,
With its many leaves,
The only thing that comforted it was the birds.
There was a bench at the bottom of its roots,
No one sat there
This was the lonely tree.

Joshua Pinchess (10)
Gayhurst School, Gerrards Cross

Squirrel

Small
Brown
Rude
Squirrel
Jumping to Pluto
Ungracefully
Sneakily
Like creamy chocolate
I'd be sad if he died
Squirrel
Rude squirrel.

Paddy Keogh (8)
Gayhurst School, Gerrards Cross

Kite

Huge
Red
Aggressive
Kite
Flying in the sky
Angrily
Grumpily
Black body
White head
Yellow beak
Kite.

William Martin (8)
Gayhurst School, Gerrards Cross

Shark

Shark,
Huge, fierce,
Destructive,
Killer of the deep,
Exploding through the water,
Powerfully and ferociously,
Like a nuclear missile,
It would be sad if you went vegetarian,
Shark!
Deadly shark!

Edwin Grimster (8)
Gayhurst School, Gerrards Cross

Shark

Stretched
Vast
Blue
Shark
Swimming through the water
Speedily
Booming
Sneaks like a robber
I would feel so unhappy if you were gone
Shark
Sneaky shark.

Ben Eastwood (8)
Gayhurst School, Gerrards Cross

Snake

Slippery
Slithering
Snake
Slipping through the grass
Slowly
Swivelling rapidly
Curving
Furious
Snake.

James Liveing (8)
Gayhurst School, Gerrards Cross

The Karate Chopper

The karate chopper
Is the strongest of the lot
He breaks all types of things
Especially his own pots
He knows what to do
When you're in trouble
When you're in jail
You will go all pale
But what he does is something amazing
This might sound weird but he breaks through bars
And runs down to get some buns.

Craig Baillie (10)
Gayhurst School, Gerrards Cross

My Grandad The Rock Star!

My grandad is a punk
He even uses hair gunk
Rocking all day
And rolling all night
He gives all the old ladies a fright
Riding around on his bike
It is a lovely red trike
Playing the guitar
You've probably guessed
He is a rock star!

Harry Cruickshank (10)
Gayhurst School, Gerrards Cross

London

London is a huge place to be,
It makes me feel as small as an ant
Next to an adult elephant.
The famous Chelsea team have their home there,
As they triumph in the Premiership each year.

London is a famous place which everyone should know.
It is like a stampede of bulls,
Beckham playing football with the latest ball.
It will make anyone proud to live there,
As you stay and stare at the amazing sights of London.

Peter Illingworth (11)
Gayhurst School, Gerrards Cross

The Spirit

A spirit floats through the foggy mist of the streets of Park Twist,
Who can tell what it is destined for?
Screaming to have its body again,
It couldn't be a spirit knocking on the door as I set foot on the
                                           dark first floor,
But as I looked through the letter box, I saw that the world was
                                          silent and still,
But as I looked at number two, I saw a spirit floating through
                                 the dark and dusty wall.

Ben Reeves (9)
Gayhurst School, Gerrards Cross

Wonders Of The Night

The owl is hooting to fill the air
The wind is blowing in my hair,
The river runs, rippling softly
Not a care anywhere.

Time goes on and one
Forever it is long,
No one asks questions of the night
Until the glimpse of light.

Moon and stars are bright
Giving their natural light,
Just enough to see the trees
Swaying softly in the breeze.

Dawn is only hours away
Until sun fills the day,
For I must leave until tomorrow
Oh, my heart fills with sorrow.

Ellie Raby-Smith (10)
Laxton Junior School, Oundle

Hurricanes

Alert! Alert!
Hurricane is found.
Katrina is coming in leaps and bounds.
Keep yourself safe and sound.

New Orleans has been warned.
. . . Vacate . . .
Or hundreds will be drowned.

Warning! Warning!
Hurricane is near.
Birds and animals flee in fear.
Trees are buffeted by the gale.
Yachts in the harbour lose their sails.
. . . Vacate . . . too late.

Aditya Shukla (10)
Laxton Junior School, Oundle

War

We're too young to remember,
Remember the horror of war,
Mud, trenches and gunfire,
Tanks, bombs, explosives galore.

Cannons, noise, damage and blood,
Tears in people's eyes,
Fear of getting shot to death,
No time for any goodbyes.

Weapons being used so much,
By people fighting for their lives,
Scrambling over dusty sand,
Tanks rolling forward in rows of fours or fives.

So that is it, these times have gone,
Are we safe for evermore?
We don't have to starve for food,
Like those before us who won these wars.

I am just so glad I'm not
A poor soldier in those times,
I am just as happy writing
And staying behind these lines.

So remember, remember those who fought,
Against their will,
Let us praise them and
Remember them still.

Kiristina Cowley (11)
Laxton Junior School, Oundle

Tadpole

Tadpole, tadpole, swimming around,
Tadpole, tadpole, not making a sound.
Tadpole, tadpole, how do you do that?
Tadpole, tadpole, quick as that!

Joshua Green (7)
Laxton Junior School, Oundle

The Tiger

Creeping through the long green grass,
She hears the warthog grunting,
Through the lake she paddles,
She hears a group of humans hunting.

Making a run for her life,
Protecting her cubs,
From the deadly sharp knife,
Growling anxiously with fear.

Surrounded by men with only two of her cubs,
That oldest cub came running at the men,
Just like a brave, young man,
He was unlucky and didn't escape, but the others ran.

The mother lay down and wept,
To say goodbye to her son,
She tried to sleep and forget that moment when he died,
But that was her son and sadly she cried.

Eliza Burgess (9)
Laxton Junior School, Oundle

When My Dad Died

When my dad died, I didn't cry, I was brave.
I felt anger like I was guilty,
I didn't like Daddy suffering with his brain tumour.
When my dad died I felt happy as well
Because I didn't see him suffering anymore.
I was confused because I didn't know
How to start a new life.
I miss my daddy's cuddles.
I miss my daddy.
When my dad died, I didn't cry, I was brave.

Phoebe McCurdy (9)
Laxton Junior School, Oundle

All At The Midnight Mansion

The doors were tattered,
The windows shattered,
All at the midnight mansion.

The floors dusty,
The door handles rusty,
All at the midnight mansion.

'The people are dead,'
The protesters said,
All at the midnight mansion.

The policeman tried,
To say that no one died,
All at the midnight mansion.

The mansion was demolished,
All in all abolished,
No more midnight mansion.

Zulfiqar-E-Aly Dooley Kachra (9)
Laxton Junior School, Oundle

The Ghouls

The ghouls, the ghouls, the spooky, scary, freaky ghouls,
They haunt people in the night.
They creep around in the dark, gloomy shadows.
There is a little one called Sam and his favourite food is ham,
There is a dad called Mad and a mum called Yum.
The big sister is called Blister and the cat is called Mat.
The people in the city said that Blister was very pretty.
Their teeth are all yellow, but sometimes Mad will bellow.
The ghouls, the ghouls, the very frightening ghouls.
The ghouls, the ghouls, the creepy ghouls.

Freya Grayson (7)
Laxton Junior School, Oundle

Autumn Leaves

Whirling, swirling on the ground
The autumn leaves
Are found.

They come from the trees
Way up there
And would make a good bed
For a bear.

And down the road, where my sister's school is,
There's a beautiful tree,
It grows next to the students, who are busy.

In the summer its leaves are so green,
But they are red in the autumn,
More red than I've ever seen.

Autumn leaves - what a wonderful thing,
Noise that is rustling,
Like the scrunching of a crisp packet,
That is going into a bin.

Whirling, swirling on the ground
The autumn leaves
Are found.

Kayla Borley (8)
Laxton Junior School, Oundle

Dog

Little dog, big dog, how wonderful you are,
Little dog, big dog, how clever you are,
Little dog, big dog, how cuddly you are,
Little dog, big dog, how playful you are.

Black Labrador, what a lovely colour you are,
White and brown spaniel, how fast you are,
Golden Labrador, how sensible you are,
Golden retriever, how soft you are.

Ben Amps (8)
Laxton Junior School, Oundle

Night

(Inspired by 'I Met At Eve' by Walter de la Mare)

Night is an evil villain
He makes me feel scared and still
Night chills me
And he always comes back, he will

His face looks twisted and wrinkled
His eyes evil but determined
His hair is grey and matted
His mouth straight and turned down at the edges

The clothes he wears are black
With little holes in places
He also wears a cape
That he throws over the Earth

He strides confidently, staring forward
To the gates of his dark castle
His voice is strict and footsteps sinister
As he slams the door on dawn.

Alexandra Tonks (10)
Laxton Junior School, Oundle

Rabbit

Rabbit, rabbit in his hutch,
Rabbit, rabbit not doing much.

Rabbit, rabbit eating his hay,
Rabbit, rabbit what do you say?

Rabbit, rabbit in his run,
Rabbit, rabbit looking at the sun.

Rabbit, rabbit chewing wood,
Rabbit, rabbit looking good.

Francesca Hooper (7)
Laxton Junior School, Oundle

The Haunted House

Slowly the door opens, *creak, creak, creak*
I tread inside carefully as the floorboards *squeak*
Cobwebs in the corner dangle low
Steadily towards the stairs I go
I sit down on a rickety chair
And I think about what could be up there
I climb the stairs which are very steep
Patterns I make in the dust with my feet
Suddenly a bat flaps its wings in the gloom
I run nervously into the nearest room
The distant moon shines little light
I wish it wasn't the middle of the night
I think I'd better go back home
I don't like being in this house alone.

Elizabeth Farrell (8)
Laxton Junior School, Oundle

Viking Attack

The Vikings are coming, fierce fighters they are,
'They are coming, they are coming,'
I said to my pa.

Dressed in mail jerkins, sword in hand,
What a frightening sight,
They are ready for a fight,
This terrible band.

The long ships head for land,
Longing to bury the Anglo-Saxons in the sand,
They murder, steal and pillage,
Leaving devastation in every village.

Tessa Berridge (10)
Laxton Junior School, Oundle

Dolphin

Dolphin, dolphin, diving up and down
When the sun's about to go down.
Singing and shining while her reflection is showing in the sea.

Dolphin, dolphin, smiling and splashing in the sea
You're beautiful and amazing
I can't stop staring, believe me.

Dolphin, dolphin, glistening and waving
All over the dark blue sea.
You're beautiful and pretty, please listen to me.

Dolphin, dolphin, looking at me,
Yes, you've noticed,
I am so happy.

Dolphin, dolphin, staring and glaring
Are you staring at me?
Now I know, oh yes I do
You are staring at me.

Mary Bletsoe (7)
Laxton Junior School, Oundle

Ladybird

Ladybird, ladybird, lying on a leaf
Waiting for your mate
Ladybird, ladybird, sitting on a log
Looking at the gate
Ladybird, ladybird, crawling along the field
Waiting for the tractors to come in
Ladybird, ladybird, with your spotty shield
In the big, long field, defending yourself
Ladybird, ladybird, fidgeting away in the hay.

Ben Learoyd (7)
Laxton Junior School, Oundle

A Picture Of Autumn

Walking on a path . . .
Trees surround me as the breeze blows across my face
Birds chirping a lovely song
Leaves twirl down with their colours gleaming in the sunlight . . .
Red, orange, yellow and brown . . .
Forming a carpet around each tree.
Whoosh as the leaves flutter up into the air!
Making comforting pictures all around me
Slowly they land on each beautiful, growing flower
Then with a flutter the leaves blow up into the sky again
Making a lovely pile for me to jump in!

Chloe Van Slyke (8)
Laxton Junior School, Oundle

Fireworks

On Bonfire Night,
The rocket firework explodes in the air,
The Catherine wheel screeches,
Spraying out sparkles,
They make rainbow colours,
Shimmering in the dark sky,
What a lovely night it is,
With such a big bang they go.

Amrish Rajdev (10)
Laxton Junior School, Oundle

Happy Heart

Yes, yes, yes, I am happy!
Life is great, each day there's a fresh, new me.
Thank you, Lord, I'm as happy as can be.
I want to sing, I want to dance,
Oh this happiness, I'm in a trance.
Oh, my happy heart.

Lauren Ferdinand (8)
Laxton Junior School, Oundle

The Seasons

The first season of the year is
Spring, spring, spring
Where flowers grow
And birds sing

Next we have got
Hot, hot summer
Where the sky is blue
And you swim in the sea
And jump with glee

Now we have
Colourful autumn
Where all the leaves
Do a beautiful dance
And fall to the ground
In the middle of France

Last, but not least
Here is white winter
Where white snow falls
And you can make snowballs
And have a *snowball* fight!

Shalinie Sriemevan (10)
Laxton Junior School, Oundle

Slugs, Snails And Millipedes

Slugs, snails and millipedes,
What does my little sister see in these?
Earwigs, ants and wriggling worms,
Better still when they squelch and squirm,
She picks up ladybirds and sometimes a woodlouse,
But these are forbidden in our house,
She can be seen in the garden lifting a stone,
A wiggling treasure she cannot leave alone,
But the animal she really desires that won't harm her,
Is a tropical, multicoloured iguana.

Molly Clayton (9)
Laxton Junior School, Oundle

Autumn

Autumn leaves, horse chestnut trees,
Conkers on the ground,
You can pick them up with ease,
There's lots to be found!

The weather's getting colder,
Turn the heating on,
The mice are getting bolder,
Now that summer's gone!

The days are getting shorter,
Fewer daylight hours,
No need to use the water,
To perk up the flowers!

Katie Orr (9)
Laxton Junior School, Oundle

Smooth Green Marble

Smooth green marble very bright
Smooth green marble catch the light

Smooth green marble rolling along
Smooth green marble not very long

Smooth green marble waiting to be picked up
Smooth green marble put in a cup

Smooth green marble found in a pot
Smooth green marble feels hot

Smooth green marble left in a hat
Smooth green marble fell on a rat.

Anna Pathak (7)
Laxton Junior School, Oundle

Pets

Pets, pets, are very, very furry,
Pets, pets, are very, very funny,
Pets, pets, are big and small,
Pets, pets, are cute and scary.

Dogs, dogs, are bouncy and strong,
Dogs, dogs, make funny noises,
Dogs, dogs, are loyal and helpful,
Dogs, dogs, are calm and old.

Cats, cats, are scared and frightened,
Cats, cats, are brown and black,
Cats, cats, are tall and short,
Cats, cats, are fat and thin.

William Sly (7)
Laxton Junior School, Oundle

Night

(Inspired by 'I Met At Eve' by Walter de la Mare)

Night is as peaceful as a flowing river
She makes me feel as safe as being wrapped up in bed
She has a face as wise as a wizard
Her big eyes are shining stars in the sky
Her mouth is as cold as frost
Her hair is as black as your pupil
She has clothes as white as thick mist
Her movement is as quick and delicate as a cat
Her words are as cool as the wind
She lives in a palace of darkness
Night invigorates me.

Lily Clayton (10)
Laxton Junior School, Oundle

Night

(Inspired by 'I Met At Eve' by Walter de la Mare)

Night is a black cat padding softly on the grass,
Night makes me feel drowsy like a sloth,
His face looks like a beautiful dark rose,
His eyes hypnotise me to sleep,
His mouth is swallowing the sun and releasing the moon,
His hair hangs like the branches of a weeping willow,
His clothes are made of dark sheep's wool,
When he moves, his cloak flows out to reveal the stars,
When he speaks the sound echoes around,
He lives far away in a deserted cottage painted black
With his black cat,
Night calms me.

Georgina Illingworth (10)
Laxton Junior School, Oundle

Night

(Inspired by 'I Met At Eve' by Walter de la Mare)

Night is a scary belief that haunts me
He makes me feel lonely and single
His face is pale, with the pride of dignity
His eyes are fiery and vicious, like a tiger
His figure thin and sly, like a panther
His hair is silvery, like the starry night
His clothes are made of ancient white silk
He glides along swiftly and silently
He lives in dreams, up above the clouds
Night is with me
Till I die!

Angus Murphy (10)
Laxton Junior School, Oundle

Night

(Inspired by 'I Met At Eve' by Walter de la Mare)

Now is the time.
Day departs
And night begins his slow, lumbering plod over Earth.

I see him.
From far away
His flowing robe trails a blanket of stars.

Ghostly children run under his cloak for asylum.
He soothes their scalps with frosty fingertips.

Haunting shadows follow him in a deathly pilgrimage.
The air is full of the moans of martyrs.

Tower of strength,
He takes my soul to a land of dreams
And rests my head on his shoulder.

Jesse Chambers (10)
Laxton Junior School, Oundle

Night

(Inspired by 'I Met At Eve' by Walter de la Mare)

Night is a spectacular friend,
She makes me feel special,
Her face gleams with stars from the midnight sky,
Her eyes shine as bright as diamonds,
Her mouth is peaceful, she does not utter a word,
Her hair swishes across the atmosphere of night,
Her clothes are made from the stars above,
When she moves, she spreads dark and a touch of kindness,
She lives on a cloud with stars and the dark,
Night is special to me.

Eve Poulter (10)
Laxton Junior School, Oundle

Amulet

(Inspired by 'Amulet' by Ted Hughes)

Inside the hungry child, the scorching desert,
Inside the scorching desert, the empty stream,
Inside the empty stream, the child's bare feet,
Inside the child's bare feet, the helpless parents,
Inside the helpless parents, the suffering children,
Inside the suffering children, the endless drought,
Inside the endless drought, the polluted water,
Inside the polluted water, the deadly diseases,
Inside the deadly diseases, the dry soil,
Inside the dry soil, the cry of hunger,
Inside the cry of hunger, the lament of love,
Inside the lament of love, the precious mud hut,
Inside the precious mud hut, the hungry child.

Reece Coles (9)
Meadowside Junior School, Kettering

Amulet

(Inspired by 'Amulet' by Ted Hughes)

Inside the hungry child, a burning sun,
Inside the scorching sun, a scorching desert,
Inside the scorching desert, a lack of water,
Inside the lack of water, the north star,
Inside the north star, a stony horizon,
Inside the stony horizon, silence,
Inside silence, a burst of hunger,
Inside the burst of hunger, a dying baby,
Inside the dying baby, the family's tears,
Inside the family's tears, people's hearts,
Inside people's hearts, a desperate loss,
Inside the desperate loss, a hungry child.

Demi Chapman (9)
Meadowside Junior School, Kettering

The Mouse's Story

I remember when my life was worth living.
Little waves of clean, fresh water would swish softly up the shore
So I could drink in peace.
Chunks of cheese were left outside for me, fresh every day.
I would dance gleefully in the soft breeze,
Not afraid to venture into places I hadn't been before.
I would juggle juicy, fresh berries,
Swim in murky ponds,
Dive into clear rivers.
It was the best ever.
But now they're all set to catch me,
I cannot venture anymore.
The water is not clean, so if I drink I will become ill.
My family are being killed on the roads.
The beautiful trees are being cut down.
My fabulous world is no longer fabulous!

Ellie Buckby (10)
Meadowside Junior School, Kettering

I Remember

I remember all the good times in the summer and spring,
Kids splishing and splashing everywhere,
Not like now.
All of the fish around,
People talking on the bench,
Not like now.
People waving as the trains zoom past.
Now nobody comes to see the trains.
Now nobody comes to play.
Fish are dying three by three,
Factories putting germs in me.
Now nobody comes here,
It's petrifying.

Jordan Coles (10)
Meadowside Junior School, Kettering

No Harvest

No harvest in Africa
No ears of corn
Only failed crops
No nutritious vegetables and fruit
Packed with healthy vitamins
We are lucky to have harvest
No harvest in Africa
No potatoes underground
No fresh vines of grapes to crush for wine
Or golden corn waving in the air
Only barren earth
They rely on us to send them grain from rich countries
So please be there to care
No harvest in Africa
Children dying every day.

Zoe Gunter (9)
Meadowside Junior School, Kettering

One Of The Difficulties Of Writing A Poem

Rain pours like a waterfall,
On rats' hats.

Rain like a waterfall pours,
On rats' hats.

A waterfall like rain pours,
On rats' hats.

Like a waterfall rain pours,
On rats' hats.

On rats' hats,
A waterfall pours like rain.

On rats' hats pours,
Rain like a waterfall.

Richard Ashcroft (10)
Meadowside Junior School, Kettering

Polar Bear's Picture

I remember when life was good
I glided across the ice
Trickling snow landing on me
Diving into water
Gulping down fish
Around me soft, white snow
Playing with my friends
The coldness coming in
Dashing through the snow
Enjoying life while I could
Eskimos were near the water
Fishing for food
There's none left
The ice is snapping
Beneath my claws
No place to play
Hunters trying to hunt me down
They capture me
In their huge nets.

Kimberley Kingsnorth (10)
Meadowside Junior School, Kettering

The Scarecrow In The Farmyard

Dressed in a farmer's ragged braces
Old straw brain sways
In a farmyard full of frosted soil.

The pigs ignore him
The chickens peck him
On the furrowed field.

The distant barn is his home
The hedges are his haystacks.

Through the windblown tree logs
The swaying branches
Sing like the cockerel.

Georgia Harrison (10)
Meadowside Junior School, Kettering

The Fish's Story

I remember when life was good.
I wriggled across the salty sea,
Splashed joyfully through coral reefs,
Danced and cartwheeled past sunken ships,
Watched seagulls soar above my head,
Fish paradise!
Octopuses were springing by,
Waving their tentacles in every possible direction,
Manatees, like ballerinas, gracefully twirled in the sunlight.
It was great! A good memory.
But only a memory.
Day by day,
Factories were built,
Rubbish everywhere I looked.
One by one,
My family members died,
Our population slowly became smaller,
Litter was my only neighbour.
Life just wasn't worth living anymore,
My fish heaven had become fish hell.

Tasha McIntyre (10)
Meadowside Junior School, Kettering

One Of The Difficulties Of Writing A Poem

Destroying the feet of the world,
Flames flare like lightning,

Flames flare,
Lightning destroying the feet of the world,

Flames flare like lightning,
Destroying the feet of the world,

Lightning flares,
Flames destroying the feet of the world.

Josh Hicks (10)
Meadowside Junior School, Kettering

The Rabbit's Story

I remember when life was good.
I dashed across fields,
Hid in burrows,
I giggled with delight as I played with my friends,
Scavenged for food at night.
I gobbled the juicy fruit
And drank the pure water.
I wore fur, like a warm coat.
I always kept it clean
And I was very proud of it.
Insects zoomed around me
And I playfully fought them.
I bounded around them,
While they tried to fight back.
It was my dream come true,
But my past has gone now,
For the greedy hunters grew,
Their guns pointed at me.
As the hunting season came,
I cowered in my burrow,
Yet the hunters still tower above me.
Just look at me now,
I have seen many beautiful transformations,
But am forced to stay in my burrow,
With a new wound every day.

Charlotte Ashworth (10)
Meadowside Junior School, Kettering

Autumn

Autumn, when the leaves float quietly past your windowpane.
Autumn, when the leaves drop slowly from the high trees.
Autumn, when the leaves spin happily to the ground.
Autumn, when the leaves turn brown and crackle with amazement.
Autumn, when the leaves fall down with a gentle blast of wind.

Bethany Clifton (9)
Putteridge Junior School, Luton

Lilli

Lilli is my cousin,
She's a little bit mad,
Sometimes she is good,
Other times she's bad.

Lilli has a pretty face
And her hair is curly,
When she stays at my house,
She always wakes up early.

Lilli can be very sweet,
But she makes a lot of noise,
When I play at her house,
She never shares her toys.

Lilli is a tantrum queen,
You may think she's trouble,
But Lilli is my special mate,
The one I love to cuddle.

Thomas Fox-Johnson (8)
Putteridge Junior School, Luton

Who Likes Rabbits?

Rabbits are cute
They leap like a cat
They're sneaky like a mouse
They're soft as a cuddly bed
They bounce like someone on a trampoline
They wiggle like a worm
They run like someone has scared them
They are as naughty as a child
They stamp like an elephant.

Angel George (8)
Putteridge Junior School, Luton

Earth

Earth is a big, round ball,
Full of wet sea and dry sand,
With rivers and a waterfall,
Of pop singers and rock bands,
      That's the Earth.

Earth is not all it seems,
People are hurt, sometimes killed,
Water is dirty, just like streams,
Some people break in, then owners are billed.
      That's the Earth.

Earth is fun, not all the time,
I love it here, but do others?
Sirens here and there stopping crime,
Families, sisters and brothers.
      That's the Earth.
      Why not come?

Amy Parkins (11)
Putteridge Junior School, Luton

The Baby Squirrel

A baby squirrel, smelly and round
Hunting for a shiny acorn.
Scamper, scamper, scamper,
The squirrel zooms,
Running is all it does.

Dig, dig, dig goes the squirrel,
Hunt, hunt, hunt go the other squirrels,
Run little squirrel, run,
All your acorns, all your nuts,
Don't let any other squirrels get them.

Please little squirrel, *stop!*

Samantha Gray (8)
Putteridge Junior School, Luton

Alien Creature

Alien creature,
This poem will tell you all about Earth.
Alien creature,
I will tell you, beginning at birth.

Alien creature,
You can go by plane to the seven wonders of the world.
Alien creature,
On that plane you will see people's hair curled.

Alien creature,
On Earth you will see fast sports cars.
Alien creature,
There are also sweets and chocolates like Mars bars.

Alien creature,
There are also things on Earth that are bad.
Alien creature,
Like war, guns and terrorists who are mad.

Alien creature,
There are crooks who burgle houses.
Alien creature,
There are also people who smoke in their lounges.

Alien creature,
So you've heard about Earth's feature.
Alien creature,
Alien creature.

Kavi Raval (10)
Putteridge Junior School, Luton

What I Want To Be

What I want to be is a ballerina
Watch me leap in the sky
I will be in a pink tutu
Up high in the sky
When I come back down
I'll leap back up again
See me in the sky all day
And that will be my day

What I want to be is a musician
I will play the piano
I will be on the piano all day long
With my piano pieces
When I am older I will be a brilliant piano player
I will be brilliant at these two things
You just wait and see!

Emily Goddard (7)
Putteridge Junior School, Luton

Hallowe'en

It's Hallow-Hallowe'en
And I'm bustin' some moves,
While you tap your shoes.

With scary costumes
And wicked dance moves.

So come along
And join in with all the fun.

Yeah, yeah.

Laxman Godhania (10)
Putteridge Junior School, Luton

SD

Super dog Stinger is always on call,
Villains, monsters and robbers,
He will catch them all.
They can commit their crime by day or night,
But Stinger will always see them
With his X-ray sight.

His super-powered cape of yellow and black,
Will put them down with a mighty smack.
No matter what the crooks try
They will always fail,
Thanks to Stinger,
The dog with his marvellous tail.

So whenever you're in trouble,
Pick up the dog and bone,
And give super dog Stinger a phone!

Hayley Watson (10)
Putteridge Junior School, Luton

My Cat Milo

My cat Milo likes to eat a lot of food,
My cat Milo likes to hunt for food,
My cat Milo likes to muck around.

My cat Milo loves to play,
My cat Milo loves to jump,
My cat Milo loves to explore.

My cat Milo hates milk,
My cat Milo hates being told off,
My cat Milo hates being shouted at,
But he makes me laugh all the time.

Danielle Gooch (8)
Putteridge Junior School, Luton

Planet Earth

We live on the planet Earth
What a beautiful planet we live on
It looks like a big, round sphere
It has big green blobs, all different shapes and sizes
This is called land
Land is surrounded by the oceans
We have to cross the oceans to get to different countries
Humans live in continents
A continent is made up of different countries
In a country we have a capital city.

We humans live on a beautiful planet
Full of great things
Things that God has made
And things that us humans have made
God has made beautiful things
Like animals, plants, forests and trees
Mountains, lakes, rivers and seas
And there are things that us humans have made
Including sports cars, The Empire State Building
The Pyramids, The Eiffel Tower and much, much more.

We humans also live in a bad world full of
Poverty, racism, suicide bombers, drugs
Alcohol and guns
We humans pray that the good things in this
World outweigh the bad.

Matthew Dawson (11)
Putteridge Junior School, Luton

Midnight Camp - Haiku

Dead of night, homesick
Not me, but eyes are staring
I hear wolves howling.

Bethany Freeman (9)
Putteridge Junior School, Luton

Millie And Presto

Presto was an elephant, he was Millie's pet,
She loved him so much,
She decided she wanted to be an elephant vet.

She played with him and taught him new tricks,
One of her favourites was picking up sticks.

He scared all of her bullies away,
And she was never troubled again after that day.

Then one day Dad shouted, 'Millie, there's a letter for you.'
She opened it to find it said: 'Wanted, elephant for new zoo'.

Millie was heartbroken, she started to cry,
She then said to Presto, 'Why did this happen, why oh why?'

Dad came upstairs, he opened Millie's door,
He then saw her crying on the bedroom floor.

Dad said, 'It's OK, you don't have to say yes,
We'll ring up the zoo and tell them you don't want to,
that will be best.'

So Dad rang the zoo and told them Millie didn't want
to give Presto away,
and Millie felt better for the rest of the day.

She then said to Presto, 'I'll never give you away to any park or zoo,
And I'd just like to say, I love you.'

Alice Kiss (10)
Putteridge Junior School, Luton

A Big, Fat Cat

A big, fat cat lives down the road,
He has a collar as big as a bone.
He is a green cat with a skinny head
And a small body with thin legs.
He scratches you all over with his sharp claws
And looking after him is such a big chore.

Hannah Lake (10)
Putteridge Junior School, Luton

Blueberry Fly

I was sitting in
The garden watching
The summer day go by,
Whilst I was eating
Some blueberry pie.
All of a sudden
A fly flew by
It had its eye
On my blueberry pie.
It should have known better
Than to eye my blueberry pie,
So I swatted it as it flew by.
I love blueberry pie,
Goodbye, hungry fly.

William Shadbolt (8)
Putteridge Junior School, Luton

Nothing

Imagine a world with no plants, no animals,
No more days and no more nights.
Imagine a world with no vehicles, no factories
And no street lights.
A world so hot that in seconds it could kill you,
A world that nobody's ever been to,
A world that you learn about at school and college,
A world that's shaped like a big, juicy orange.
But this is no world, this is a big ball of fire.
This is millions of times bigger and much, much brighter.
This is the *sun.*

Eleanor Hudson (9)
Putteridge Junior School, Luton

Dino The Super

Dinaman's dinosaur, he's the best
Helping pets under stress
Black suit with a matching hat
He's smarter than that Robin's bat

Dinaman's dinosaur, with gigantic feet
He never sits still on his seat
He doesn't really get in the way
Well, that's what the people say

Better than Batman's robin
Faster than Robin's bat
Bigger than Spiderman's spider
Funkier than Catwoman's cat

He helps Dinaman save the day
Yes, he does have super powers by the way
Dino is his name
You can count on him to save the day.

Abigail Parry (11)
Putteridge Junior School, Luton

Football!

I like it because it's fun,
I like it because I see my friends,
I like it because it keeps me fit,
I like it because I get better at it every day,
I like it because I put a lot of effort into it.

I like football a lot,
I like it so much that I play for a team,
I like playing sport, football's the best,
I like Chelsea Football Club,
They're better than the rest!

Matthew Dimmock (8)
Putteridge Junior School, Luton

The Home Of Humans Is Earth

The home of humans is Earth,
There are bombers, there are drugs,
There are bad occasions
And there are thugs.

The home of humans is Earth,
There is illness, there is war,
There are very bad things,
Like pollution and the poor.

The home of humans is Earth,
There is good, there is bad,
There are many different feelings,
Like being happy, like being sad.

The home of humans is Earth,
There are ships, there are jets,
There are good things,
Like animals and pets.

The home of humans is Earth,
There is food, there is water,
There are very bad people,
There are killers, there is slaughter.

Some people try to give money to the needy,
But some people are really greedy.

This is what Earth is like!

Sammy-Jo McGrath (11)
Putteridge Junior School, Luton

Jack The Little Dog

Jack is a little dog,
He's brown and white.
He chased a nasty cat
And then he gave it a fright.

Samantha Weaver (8)
Putteridge Junior School, Luton

In The Playground

In the playground . . .

Philip is spinning,
Patrick's pushing,
Ross is kicking,
Russell's rushing.

Rachel's running,
Tina's tripping,
Helen's hopping,
Sarah's skipping.

Chris is chasing,
Claire is dodging,
Ben is bumping,
James is jogging.

Simon's standing,
Steven's staring,
Elle's eating,
Samantha's sharing.

Sally's shoving,
Helen's hugging,
Leroy's reading,
Tamzin's tugging.

Manisha Bajaj (10)
Putteridge Junior School, Luton

The Hyena

I'm a hyena, I live in the Savannah,
I'm a hyena, I come out at night,
I hunt impala, I give them a fright,
I'm a hyena, I laugh really loud,
I'm a hyena, I live underground,
I'm a hyena, I live in a pack,
I'm a hyena, I eat scraps,
I'm a hyena, the strongest in the land.

Kim Hughes (8)
Putteridge Junior School, Luton

Henry VIII

Henry VIII was fat and stubborn,
It always was his way.
He hunted wild pigs and boar
And other animals that were poor.
He liked dancing,
He liked eating,
He was *rich!*
Henry VIII was very rich,
He was very titchy,
He wore rich clothes,
He didn't wear bows.
He had his wives,
They weren't in fives,
They weren't in fives!
Henry VIII was fat and stubborn,
It always was his way.
He hunted wild pigs and boar
And other animals that were poor.
He liked dancing,
He liked eating,
He liked money,
He was rich, he was rich!

Nina Kiva (8)
Putteridge Junior School, Luton

I'm On My Way To An Exciting Day At Legoland

It was a lovely October's day,
I was on my way.
The last time I went it was May,
I arrived that day.
I passed my way through the crowds,
I saw a fight,
So I thought I might run away.
I was a boaster,
So I thought I might go on a roller coaster.

Ellie Chittenden (8)
Putteridge Junior School, Luton

This Is Earth

This is Earth,
Of good, of bad,
Of history and war,
Of crooks and trees
And of course the law

This is Earth,
Of fashion, of friends,
Of sports and drugs,
Of music and money
And of course the bugs

This is Earth,
Of food, of drink,
Of roads and pollution,
Of fire and water
And of course no solution

Earth is excellent.

Megan Close (10)
Putteridge Junior School, Luton

Sharks

Sharks are big
Sharks are blue
And can chase after you.

Sharks are fierce
Sharks are cool
And don't live in your swimming pool.

Sharks are good
Sharks are bad
Sharks have teeth
Unlike Grandad!

Katie Riviere (8)
Putteridge Junior School, Luton

Friends Or Foes?

Friends are always there for you,
Friends are helpful when you're blue.
Friends care in all cases,
Friends treat you to nice places.

Foes are tough,
Foes are rough.
Foes hit out,
Foes shout!

Friends or foes?
Foes or friends?
Friendship endures,
Foes entrap.

Friends or foes?

Charlie Pepper (10)
Putteridge Junior School, Luton

My Dog Dudley

My dog Dudley
Is cute, friendly
And cuddly.

He loves going on walks,
Oh, how I wish he could talk.

His tail wags, I never see it stop,
He eats so fast, I think he will pop.

He is growing so fast,
The puppy stage will never last.

Hannah Kiss (9)
Putteridge Junior School, Luton

Water Waves

Rushing, splashing water waves
As the day goes past
I told my friend to look at the waves
As they go so fast.
Me and my friend went into the sea
Running oh so bold
But as we reached the water's edge
We found it freezing cold.
As we stood in the water
A big wave came along
And knocked us over, *splash!* we went!
We never knew waves were so strong.
Drowned and wet we're going home now
To dry ourselves with a nice warm towel.

Matthew Chamberlain (8)
Putteridge Junior School, Luton

Fishing

When my dad and I go fishing,
We are always wishing,
For a great big carp to take the bait,
Oh my goodness, we have to wait,
Such a long time with nothing to do,
Except watch the ducks swim around in twos,
Suddenly I feel a tug on the line,
I think this is going to be just fine,
I reel it in and to my surprise,
A stinky old boot all covered in flies!

Jamie Loveday (9)
Putteridge Junior School, Luton

The Good And Bad Things About Earth

You get food,
You get drink,
You get water,
You get oxygen.

You get birthdays,
You get Christmas,
You get Easter,
You get fireworks night.

But . . .
There is war,
There is starvation,
There is poverty.

There are drugs,
There is pollution,
There are cigarettes,
There are diseases.

So would you like to come to Earth?

Katy Risbridger (10)
Putteridge Junior School, Luton

The Splash

We went swimming today,
We splashed and played
And made big waves.
We dived into blue water,
We jumped and surfed on floats,
We used them just like boats.
I skidded into deep, choppy water
And my sister roared with laughter.

Bradley Andrews (8)
Putteridge Junior School, Luton

In The Future

In the future I would like:
Animals that talk,
Robots that walk
And cars that can fly,
High up in the sky.

In the future in space I would like:
A luxury home,
With a roof like a dome,
And when you want to go somewhere,
You ride on the back of an alien bear.

In the future in the sea I would like:
To go below the sea floor,
And find the bones of a dinosaur,
Oil can be transported to New York's refinery,
In thousands of bottles sealed with thousands of corks.
Now this poem has come to an end,
Can you make this come true?
I can't, can you?

Sam Glenister (9)
Putteridge Junior School, Luton

Cats

I have a cat, it's fast, soft and greedy.
She's my cat called Millie,
She's as fast as the wind,
Quiet as a mouse
And greedy as a pig.
She's multicoloured,
Gentle and cuddly.
She is clean as ever,
Small as a stone
And she's lazy you see.

Daniel Auburn (8)
Putteridge Junior School, Luton

When I'm Older

When I'm older I want to be
A famous cricketer which you can see
Driving sixes, cutting fours
Smashing windows and pavilion doors
I'll bowl leg spin, I'll get them out
When I do that, they'll scream and shout
I'll be better than Shane Warne, I will be
You come and watch me, then you'll see

When I'm older I want to be
A famous musician which you can see
Electric guitars, a big set of drums
Holding a microphone with my fingers and thumbs
I'll make them shout and clap their hands
While I'm singing in my rock band
I'll be better than U2, I will be
You come and watch me, then you'll see

When I'm older I want to be
A famous author who you can read
Adventures, characters who can do magic
Some things that are really tragic
People might read my books and say with a smile,
'This book I bought was really worthwhile'
I would be better than Roald Dahl, I'd be
You read my books and then you'll see

When I'm older I want to be
A famous poet who you can read
Poems about you, poems about me
Poems even like this maybe
Sometimes a poet who always makes jokes
Even a poet who writes old people's folk
I'd be better than TS Elliot, I'd be
You read my poems and then you'll see.

Oliver Goddard (9)
Putteridge Junior School, Luton

The Future

When I think about the future . . . I think:
Eating chocolate, biscuits and sweets all the time,
Staying up late all night watching telly,
Climbing trees in other people's gardens,
Zooming about in my brand new car,
Spending money on pretty clothes,
Having fun in Disneyland,
Living in a castle right by a sandy beach,
Going shopping and buying useless things,
Like flowerpots and pencils and other non-interesting things,
Never going to the doctors or work,
Oh, what fun it would be!
But then it all comes to an end,
And that's when I realise,
I will have a great responsibility,
Paying bills and taxes,
Getting a job and earning money,
Getting a husband and having children,
Making sure I get enough sleep,
Going to the doctor and the dentist,
Setting a good example for children and younger people,
Eating healthy food and having a good diet,
Buying important things like clothes, food, things for the house, and
Doing housework,
So much to do!
I don't think I'll be able to take it!
Why can't it be more fun and exciting like the earlier years?

Helena Gookey (9)
Putteridge Junior School, Luton

David Beckham And The Ferrari Enzo

(Based on 'The Walrus and the Carpenter' by Lewis Carroll)

The sun was shining on the football pitch,
Shining with all his might,
He did his very best to make
The billows smooth and bright,
And this was odd, because it was,
The middle of the night.

The moon was shining sulkily,
Because she thought the sun,
Had got no right to be there,
After the day was done.
'It's very rude of him,' she said,
'To come and spoil the fun.'

David Beckham and the Ferrari Enzo,
Were riding close at hand,
The Ferrari Enzo's engine,
Was revving up quite grand.
And all of a sudden the engine,
Was put to the ultimate test,
On the beautiful green grass brand.

'The time has come,' David said,
'To talk of many things,
Of football boots and football kits
And anything with bling,
And why the football pitch is green
And whether Ferraris have wings.'

Stephanie Little (10)
Putteridge Junior School, Luton

Earth

Earth is a really big place,
With loads and loads of people.
There are good things and bad things,
This is the Earth.

The bad things are racism,
Terrorists and diseases,
Also cigarettes and drugs,
This is the Earth.

The good things are oxygen,
Food and drink,
Also families and friends,
This is the Earth.

This is the Earth,
This is the Earth.

Louie Penfold (10)
Putteridge Junior School, Luton

Our Planet Is Called Earth

Our planet is called Earth
We have football pitches and turf
We have sweets and schools
And a lot of rules

Our planet is called Earth
We have seas to surf
We have TV and toys
And a lot of boys

Our planet is called Earth
We have dummies and birth
We have curtains and beds
And a lot of people dead.

Our planet is called Earth.

Michaella Beckwith (10)
Putteridge Junior School, Luton

My White Horse

I saw my white horse
I see it every day
I saw my white horse
It was eating the hay.

My beautiful white horse
It likes to run free
I chase it sometimes
It chases me.

Beauty is fine
He has a lovely mane
Beauty is fine
So I chose that name.

He gallops along alone every day
My horse is so lonely, it wants to play
I come to see him
As much as I like
So sometimes I come and ride
On my bike.

Joe Tucker (8)
Putteridge Junior School, Luton

What Does The Future Bring?

What does the future bring?
Summer, autumn, winter, spring.
A day of sunshine, a night of snow
Sometimes we never know.
Teenage years,
Hopes and fears,
Examinations,
Celebrations,
What does the future bring?
No one knows, that's one sure thing.

Amy Pollard (10)
Putteridge Junior School, Luton

Us Humans

To you things up in space,
I'm telling you about this place,
There are some good things,
But some bad things,
This place is called Earth.

On Earth it is quite big,
But compared to other planets, it's small,
There are tasty foods like sweets and pizza,
But they are fattening.
There are healthy foods like vegetables,
But they taste a bit yucky!

There are other things like oxygen,
It's an essential thing to us,
We could not live without it,
We need food and water to live,
But we most of all need oxygen.

There are bad things too, like war,
War is when humans fight,
There is poverty which is when people are poor,
They beg for money on the street,
They need it to get back on their feet.

This is what it's like on Earth!

Michael Jones (10)
Putteridge Junior School, Luton

Planets

There were nine planets in the solar system,
But now there are ten.
The planets are all different.
Mercury, nearest the sun, is small and hot
Then Venus, Earth and Mars are rocky and cooler.
Beyond them, Jupiter, Saturn, Uranus and Neptune are large and cold,
Whilst Pluto is tiny and icy.
Sedna is the latest planet to be discovered.

Pratik Shah (8)
Putteridge Junior School, Luton

Autumn Time

All the leaves are falling down,
Dancing, swirling to the ground,
Bright, gleaming and golden brown,
There is a stillness about the town.

All the trees are brown and bare,
Autumn's come, I do declare,
Burning smells are in the air,
And warmer clothes we have to wear!

Alisha Seera (8)
Putteridge Junior School, Luton

Fantasy

Unicorns and fairies are fantasy creatures
They are beautiful and have lovely features
They are not real as we all know
But in our dreams we see them so

Unicorns and their magical horns
Fly in the air till daylight dawns
Fairies with their see-through wings
Dancing round the flowers they sing.

Lauren James (8)
Putteridge Junior School, Luton

Ginny And Fred

I have two cats called Ginny and Fred,
They like to sleep with me on my bed.
Ginny's a tabby and Fred is shiny black,
When they see a mouse they're sure to attack.
Both of them like to chase bits of string,
My big brother, Daniel, likes to sing.
This is my super, wicked rap,
So everybody here please give me a clap.

Alex Hayward (8)
Putteridge Junior School, Luton

Goal

'Goal, goal!' my fans did cry,
I watched as the ball whizzed in the sky.
I smiled as it shot to the back of the net,
I spotted a defender, my target was set.
I ran up to him with all my might,
I was sure I was gonna score tonight.
As the ball slowly passed to my feet,
I knew this was a team I had to beat.
In my clean, new kit I felt so proud,
All I wanted to do was please the crowd.
The goalie was big, but I wasn't scared,
'Penalty! Penalty!' the ref declared.
I took up my space on the penalty spot,
I'm gonna give this kick all I've got.
It flew past the keeper and into the goal,
I love football, it's in my soul.
Football's brilliant, football's the best,
After this game I need a long rest.

Jack Hattle (9)
Putteridge Junior School, Luton

The Back To Front Life Of A Dog

Wake up early on a Sunday morning,
Must take my human for a walk in the park,
Don't forget to feed it some nice, tasty doggy biscuits,
While I have yummy bacon and eggs,
Curled up on the sofa watching a football match,
Whilst out in the garden the human plays with a ball,
It's starting to get late now,
So I snuggle down in bed,
The human's asleep in its basket,
Cuddling big, furry ted.

Amy Gardner (9)
Putteridge Junior School, Luton

The Weather

Weather can be wonderful
Weather can be cruel
Sometimes it frightens you
Sometimes it amazes you.
Thunder, lightning, hail and more
White little drops of snow
Hop and dance to the ground.
Big, fluffy clouds come to rest in the sky
Then pour rain down to the ground.
Hurricanes and thunderstorms I like to watch
From the safety of my bedroom window.
Sun shines so bright
It also brings a lovely sight.
The clouds also show signs of storms
All types of weather in the sky
Waiting to drop down to Earth.

Yasmin Kreft (8)
Putteridge Junior School, Luton

Planet Earth

Oxygen is good,
Pollution is bad,
Food is good,
Food poisoning is bad,
Religion can be good,
Racism is bad,
Holidays in hot countries are good,
Malaria in hot countries is bad,
Civilisation is good,
Habitat destruction is bad,
In the west people throw food away,
In many parts of Africa people don't have food to eat,
In some countries it isn't safe to go out the door,
In some countries people don't have a door to go out,
So would you want to come to Earth?

Sophie Webb (10)
Putteridge Junior School, Luton

The Earth

To everyone that lives in space
Earth is a very weird place
With lots of girls and boys
That love sweets, chocolate and toys
They like TV because it's cool
But they hate school!
They like sports and games and things like that
They like Hallowe'en with blood and bats.

But there are bad things on Earth
People don't have everything
Like food and drink
There are bombers, guns and war
And much more!
The Earth is dangerous and bad
It can be very sad.

Earth is good and bad
It can be happy and sad
People have friends
A list that never ends!
Earth is not as bad as it seems
There are good things
Like when we dream!

Kellyanne Batchelor (10)
Putteridge Junior School, Luton

Kim Possible

I like Kim Possible,
She's impossible to defeat,
She's incredible and strong,
She's ultra cool,
But she's not a fool,
She's always late for class,
Although she can't pass the test,
She's very clever!

Harkirit Rayatt (8)
Putteridge Junior School, Luton

Earth

To everyone up in space,
Humans like to race,
In sports cars and motorbikes,
We also have little trikes.

Sweets are the best,
In bed we have a rest,
Christmas is really fun,
In winter we have no sun.

TV is really cool,
Humans are big and small,
Hi-tech products are the type,
That make you hype, hype.

War is full of blood,
And bullies throw mud,
People do drugs,
And steal mugs.

Animals are good and bad,
If you get bitten you will be sad,
Racism is disrespect,
So just give a little respect.

So would you come to planet Earth?

Sam Ferrell (10)
Putteridge Junior School, Luton

Fire

Fire, fire, burning bright,
Keeps us warm through the night.
On the fire, sticks I throw,
To keep the orange-yellow glow.
On a fire, on a stick,
I cook marshmallows very quick.
Songs are sung, stories are read,
Until it's time to go to bed.

Sophie Smith (8)
Putteridge Junior School, Luton

What Means The Most Is . . .

What means the most is family!
What means the least is gel,
But all we need is water,
Not Christmas presents and sweets.

What means the most is your home!
What means the least is chocolate,
But all we need are friends,
Not PS2 games and TV.

What means the most is happiness!
What means the least is terrorism,
But all we need is good health,
Not hi-tech and fancy clothes.

So all we need is:
Family,
Happiness,
Home,
Friends,
Food,
Drink
And yourself!

Louis Horan (10)
Putteridge Junior School, Luton

A Big Fish Wish

There was once a big fish,
Who had a big wish,
Which was to swim in the sea.
But that big fish,
Who had a big wish,
Did not get his wish,
Because he was fried in a dish
And was sold in a shop called
'A fish in a dish'.

Adam Joyce (8)
Putteridge Junior School, Luton

My Cat, Chelsea

I have a cat called Chelsea,
She really is quite old,
She's a lovely little tabby
Who never does as she's told.

She has green eyes,
Ears that are so fluffy,
She runs around in the garden
And comes back so scruffy.

Some people are scared of her,
When she hisses at them,
But when she's with me,
She'll just sit and purr,
That's my cat, Chelsea.

Amber Godfrey (8)
Putteridge Junior School, Luton

The Old Man

The old man down my street
Has very peculiar feet.
One wooden
The other real.
I asked him one day,
'How does it feel
And wouldn't you rather both of them real?'
He laughed and smiled
And then he said,
'I would rather one wooden,
I could have been dead.'

Jay Clarke (8)
Putteridge Junior School, Luton

The World

Bad are drugs
Good is water
Bad are guns
Good are families
Bad is disease
Good are birthdays

Don't do bad
Do good

Bad is racism
Good are friends
Bad is pollution
Good is electricity
Bad are terrorists
Good is yourself.

Look after the world.

Sam Gale (11)
Putteridge Junior School, Luton

Sharks

Sharks are aggressive, powerful predators,
They rip up prey with haste.
They're
Fierce,
Mean,
Animals.
They're kings of the sea.
Fins rise slowly out of the water
And you know you're being watched.
They hunt and kill
And you feel afraid.

Sebastian Cooper (8)
Putteridge Junior School, Luton

Our World

A family, some friends
Help you along in this world
Food is smooth, food is lumpy
Apples smooth, pasta bumpy

We breathe in oxygen
Trees breathe it out
Trees breathe in carbon dioxide
So we must breathe it out

There's war, dying, guns
The world can be at shame
Think about the day the world can have
The racism about other religions

There are so many things
About this world
We really need to change
But it's *cool!*

Kayley-Anne Lee (10)
Putteridge Junior School, Luton

Seashore

Sandy shore and salty seaweed,
Rocks and cockleshells,
Pebbles round and salty,
And the sea all blue and green.

Sun on the wavy water,
The sea flying all about,
Footprints in the sand - ripples,
All the scouts shout.

Surfers against the sunshine,
The sea shouting, 'Hello,'
Castles in the sand,
Around the wind blows.

Miraj Shah (8)
Putteridge Junior School, Luton

The Horse

Gallop my horse, gallop,
With your black tail flying back,
Your hooves clipping on the cornfield,
Carry on zooming around this field,
I urge you on, as it's such fun,
I squeeze my legs on your body,
To keep you moving on,
So keep on galloping I plead,
Gallop, gallop please, my black horse,
Night is so fast you can barely see her move,
Let the reins go free,
Grip onto the saddle,
As you zoom like a shooting star,
My beautiful horse Night,
Carry on zooming into the night,
Where the stars twinkle,
As you go around this cornfield,
Night is as black as a night sky.

Sophie Risbridger (8)
Putteridge Junior School, Luton

Earth

The Earth is a big place,
The Earth is surrounded by space,
With humans working every day,
We have taxes and bills we have to pay,
With sports cars and speedboats,
With carnivals with colourful floats,
With tanks and battleships used for war,
With wild animals and lions that roar,
With celebrations and parties full of fun,
With people in poverty and in a slum,
With disease and suffering,
With poor people and rich ones with bling,
With sport and education and everyone.

Russell Attwood (10)
Putteridge Junior School, Luton

The Car And The Mechanic

(Based on 'The Walrus and the Carpenter' by Lewis Carroll)

The sun was shining on the bonnet,
Shining with all his might,
He did his very best to make
The bonnet shiny and bright -
And this was odd, because it was,
The middle of the night.

The moon was shining sulkily,
Because she thought the sun
Had got no business to be there
After the day was done -
'It's very rude of him,' she said,
'To come and spoil the fun!'

The car and the mechanic,
Were working close at hand,
They wept like anything because,
The gearbox was full of sand.
'If this problem cleared away,
It surely would be grand!'

'The time has come,' the mechanic said,
'To work on many things:
On tyres and wheels and greasy wax,
On steering wheels - and things.
And why the engine is boiling hot,
And whether cars need springs!'

The car ceased to sob,
The mechanic ceased to weep,
They'd finished all the jobs
And they lay down to sleep.
And of their craft and workmanship,
The engine seemed to reap.

William Finnie (11) & Miheer Soni (10)
Putteridge Junior School, Luton

The Lion And The Zookeeper

(Based on 'The Walrus and the Carpenter' by Lewis Carroll)

The sun was shining on the zoo,
Shining with all its might,
He did his very best to make,
The animals happy and bright -
And this was odd, because it was,
The middle of the night.

The moon was shining sulkily,
Because she thought the sun,
Had no business to be there,
After the day was done.
'It's very rude of him,' she said,
'To come and spoil the fun.'

The zookeeper was hungry as could be,
But the lion was fine as fine,
There was no rain,
For there were no clouds,
'Come, let's go and dine,'
The zookeeper said,
'That sounds simply divine.'

'The time has come,' the zookeeper said,
'To talk of many things,
Of shoes - ships - and sealing wax -
Of cabbages and kings -
And why the sea is boiling hot -
And whether pigs have wings!'

The lion he ceased to sob,
The zookeeper ceased to weep,
They'd finished all the bread and cream
And had lain down to sleep,
And of their greediness and selfishness,
Their punishment they had to keep.

Kendall Bull (10) & Lewis Hills (10)
Putteridge Junior School, Luton

World Poem

There are a lot of things that humans can do,
That could be good or bad - you choose.
There are a lot of bad things to say,
Like when people are dying each day.

There are a lot of diseases like AIDS and cancer,
But some people think they have the answer.
They are just asking for some money,
In more than one way - some of them funny!

But there are a lot of things that are good as well,
The seven wonders of the world can be just swell.
Food and water, some people have plenty,
Food or starvation - you decide -
Or war and pollution - countries collide.

Lewis Synan-Jones (10)
Putteridge Junior School, Luton

Earth

The Earth is a strange place,
The Earth has food and drink,
The Earth is not all good,
The Earth is not all bad.

Our Earth has lots of things,
Our Earth has buildings, trees and animals,
Our Earth has poverty, war and bombers,
Our Earth has people, families and friends.

When you come to Earth we can go bowling,
When you come to Earth we can go swimming,
When you come to Earth we can go hiking,
When you come to Earth we can have fun!

So would you like to come to Earth?

Megan Ward (10)
Putteridge Junior School, Luton

The Pop Singer And The Rock Band

(Based on 'The Walrus and the Carpenter' by Lewis Carroll)

The sun was shining on the stage,
Shining with all his might,
He did his very best to make,
The record smooth and bright -
And this was very odd because it was,
The middle of the night.

The singer was singing sulkily,
Because he thought the band,
Had no business to be there,
He wanted to earn a grand.
'Why are you here?' sung the singer.
The band replied, 'We thought you needed a hand.'

'The time has come,' the singer sang,
'To talk of many things,
Of music, sound and money -
Of fans, microphones and blings,
And why we argue all the time.'
The crowd went silent and the phone went *ding*.

At the end the band and singer,
Were walking close together,
Singing different tunes,
But they didn't know whether,
They would be friends or not,
Or it would last forever.

Mandla Bandama (11)
Putteridge Junior School, Luton

The Earth

The Earth is a big human home,
Where humans are all shapes and sizes,
They work together all the time,
For the good or the crime.

All the time they're helping out,
Trying to chuck poverty out,
There are the good times and the bad,
Like building the seven wonders, that's mad.

Suddenly there is a war because of drugs,
Racism and very much more,
We fight over stupid things,
Which could be working out like this;
Trading, buying, or maybe selling.

We always take things for granted,
Like water, oxygen and even air,
Also food, drink and houses.

This world is full of terrorists,
Who always solve stuff with their fists,
Stealing, taking without asking
And never doing right.

We're humans, we're humans
And that's that!

Patrick Frater-Loughlin (10)
Putteridge Junior School, Luton

My Hamster

Her name is Alex.
She's cute and cuddly
When she sticks her nose out.
She's got a white nose
And she is grey up to her tum.
She has a white tummy
And grey back legs.
Also, she's completely tame.
Alex runs on my hands
And on my arm.
When too many people try to hold her,
She starts to hoard food.
When we went on holiday,
She bit the plastic in her cage.
I love my hamster Alex.

Ross Arnold (8)
Putteridge Junior School, Luton

Our Home: Earth

The Earth is the home of humans,
We have good and bad things,
We have vital food and water,
But we also have slaughter.
We have safe homes
And we also have mobile phones,
We have bad and good bugs
And bad and good drugs.
We have lots of celebrations like
Easter, Christmas and everything!
But pollution smells *pong, ping!*
We don't think negative,
Always positive!
This is what Earth is like!

David Lapushner (10)
Putteridge Junior School, Luton

The Earth

The Earth is a strange place,
Things happen every day,
It could be good, it could be bad,
In any kind of way.

Most people have homes, most people have families
And games to play with a friend,
They could be good friends or maybe not,
Some last till the end.

Everyone should have food and drink,
To help them to survive,
Without most things we have today,
We probably wouldn't be alive.

Unfortunately, we have poverty,
We have diseases and war,
We hope to get rid of them one day,
But we just keep getting more.

So there is the Earth for you,
Just think about it,
Do you like it? Do you not?
If you do, come and visit.

Rhys O'Nions (10)
Putteridge Junior School, Luton

Vikings

The Vikings were big, hairy, ferocious killers,
They would rather be robbers than normal people.
They took anything they fancied,
The harmless Vikings always stayed at home.

They killed the biggest animal in the world,
The harmless Vikings grew crops to live,
They had dangerous weapons,
They were the vicious Vikings.

Harry Burnham (8)
Putteridge Junior School, Luton

About Earth

The Earth is filled with lots of good things,
The Earth is filled with lots of bad things,
The Earth is filled with love and laughter,
The Earth is filled with murder and war.

The Earth is filled with millions of people,
The Earth is filled with millions of creatures,
The Earth is filled with lots of living things,
The Earth is filled with lots of dead things.

The Earth is filled with rich countries,
The Earth is filled with poor countries,
The Earth is filled with hunger and starvation,
The Earth is filled with full tummies and delicious treats.

Raja Birring (10)
Putteridge Junior School, Luton

I Love Food

I love food, it tastes go good,
From crunchy carrots to sloppy soup,
Freezing ice cream to spicy, hot curry,
It all goes well in my little tummy.

I love food, it smells so nice,
To chicken, herbs and spice,
Slurping, burping, gulping, slopping,
My belly hurting.

I love food, but not too much,
Leave it an hour and I'll have the power
For the most important part,
Chocolate! Yum-yum!

Ashleigh Bowler (8)
Putteridge Junior School, Luton

All About Cats

Cats are cuddly and cute
And some of them are black like a bat.
Cats are lazy and good at running
And of course, some of them are fat!
Cats like to catch birds.
Cats are furry like a rabbit.
Cats are cheeky because they dribble on your bed.
Cats are naughty because they go in other people's gardens.
I like cats!

Charlie Jeycock (8)
Putteridge Junior School, Luton

Sharks

Swimming under the sea is your worst nightmare,
Never a dream.
Chomping away at his favourite prey,
Staring deeply at me like a crazed sea monster.
Seals start to fight,
But you'll never get away when you get the bite,
So the victim you will be.
So watch out!
I hope it won't be me.

George Harris (8)
Putteridge Junior School, Luton

My Rabbit

My rabbit runs.
My rabbit jumps and digs holes in the ground.
She's a job to find because I can't see her.
She is all just a blur.
She's running round and round somewhere,
So I leave a trail for her to follow
And it will lead her to her hutch.

Alanta Castleman (8)
Putteridge Junior School, Luton

Swimming

I enjoy swimming, it's fun
And this is what it is about.
It's normally fun.
Sometimes we tumble, sometimes we do not.
I like doing butterfly, but sometimes I do not.
I like swimming, sometimes I like breaststroke.
It's normally really fun to swim,
So have a go and try not to sink.
It takes quite a long time to practise,
So just try!
I learnt for three years,
That is a long time, isn't it?
But it's my favourite sport!

Ashley Purdy (8)
Putteridge Junior School, Luton

My Holiday

Candyfloss - delicious, joyful and fun.
You see the sea and it is salty and wet,
With waves bigger than the classroom.
Funfair, funfair, so great.
There's the big wheel and spinning cups,
Don't be so glum, sad, stroppy,
Let's have some fun,
Buy candyfloss,
Go to the funfair.
Let's have some fun!

Rebecca Carter (8)
Putteridge Junior School, Luton

Friendship

Friendship, friendship everywhere,
Having fun and playing games.
Friendship, friendship everywhere,
People laughing and talking everywhere.
People say that friendship is a strong thing
And I say it is.
Friendship is when people care for each other.
Friendship is when people make each other laugh.
Friendship is when people are kind to each other.
Friendship is when you make each other laugh because you're sad.
Friendship, friendship, comes to everyone
And everyone has got a friend out there.
Friendship is strong
And it can never break out of the world.

Mohammed Ibara Ali Razaq (9)
Putteridge Junior School, Luton

Countdown

10 My name is Captain Ben
 9 All the systems are fine
 8 Release the brake
 7 The ship points to Heaven
 6 I'm feeling sick
 5 But feeling very alive
 4 The engines give a roar
 3 Space we will soon see
 2 We will be going very soon
 1 This will be fun
 0 Blast off!

Bradley Essex (8)
Putteridge Junior School, Luton

Football

When you play football,
You have to run.
You have to be skilful,
You have to be powerful,
You have to win.
You especially have to pass the ball,
So you'd better do all these things
To play football,
Finally, if you want to be a professional
You should work very hard to be a winner.

Yasser Thamer (8)
Putteridge Junior School, Luton

Anger

Anger is spooky red and deadly black
It tastes like soggy crisps and sour milk
It smells like dripping blood in a stinking sewer
It looks like lumpy vomit and burning flames
It sounds like people screaming and tigers roaring
Anger makes me furious.

Paul Goddard (9)
St Mary Magdalene Catholic Primary School, Milton Keynes

Jealousy

Jealousy is gut-green and snotty yellow.
It tastes like sour lemon and mouldy milk.
It smells like rotting cheese in an old maggot fridge.
It looks like purple flashes and nasty pictures.
It sounds like annoying laughs and loud screaming.
Jealousy makes me *angry*.

Drew Hennessy (10)
St Mary Magdalene Catholic Primary School, Milton Keynes

Love

Love is marshmallow pink and rosy-red.
It tastes like delicious chocolates
And succulent toffees.
It looks like two people dancing
On a hot sunset night.
It sounds like people singing
At a wedding.
Love makes me feel special.

Melanie Commey (9)
St Mary Magdalene Catholic Primary School, Milton Keynes

Love

Love is rose-red and ribbon-pink.
It tastes like chocolate melting on your tongue.
It smells like flowers just arriving on your doorstep.
It looks like hugs and kisses.
It sounds like chiming church bells ringing.
Love makes me *melt.*

Chelsea Coltart (9)
St Mary Magdalene Catholic Primary School, Milton Keynes

Anger

Anger is gulping green and shivering red.
It tastes like slimy slugs in a cupboard.
It looks like smelly socks and rotten milk.
It sounds like angry people and someone screaming.
Anger makes me scream.

Amber Sayles (9)
St Mary Magdalene Catholic Primary School, Milton Keynes

Missing You

When I'm missing you, I'm like a bird with no wings.
When I'm missing you, I'm like a river with no water.
When I'm missing you, I'm like a tongue with no taste.
When I'm missing you, I'm like a book with no words.
When I'm missing you, I'm like a friend with no friends.
When I'm missing you, I'm like a design with no pattern.
When I'm missing you, I'm like a rose with no petals.
When I'm missing you, I'm like a song with no tune.

Oyinkansola Fowowe (9)
St Mary Magdalene Catholic Primary School, Milton Keynes

Love

Love is rose-red and snow-white
It tastes like Galaxy bar
It smells like sweet flowers
Love is love
It looks like roses and a lovely poem
It sounds like children laughing
Love makes me feel cuddly.

Kaiya Feeney (9)
St Mary Magdalene Catholic Primary School, Milton Keynes

There Was An Old Lady Called Jane

There was an old lady called Jane,
Who was a bit of a pain,
She went to the pub
And ate lots of grub,
And got stuck on the end of the chain.

Bethany Conway (9)
St Mary Magdalene Catholic Primary School, Milton Keynes

Love

Love is creamy pink and purple violets.
It tastes like candyfloss on a stick.
It smells like the finest perfume
Made from the pinkest roses.
It looks like Cupid's arrows
Beaming down from the sky.
It looks like a Valentine's card
With love everywhere.
It sounds like birds singing in a tree
On a spring day.

Love makes me *warm inside*.

Fraser Green (9)
St Mary Magdalene Catholic Primary School, Milton Keynes

There Was An Old Man From Kent

There was an old man from Kent,
Who went and stayed in a tent.
He was very crazy,
At the same time lazy
And gave up bananas for Lent.

Jonathan Vines (9)
St Mary Magdalene Catholic Primary School, Milton Keynes

There Was A Young Boy Called Sam

There was a young boy called Sam,
He came from the planet Jam,
He did not like Joe,
'Cause he had a big toe,
So he hit it with a *bam!*

Alex Miles (9)
St Mary Magdalene Catholic Primary School, Milton Keynes

Love

Love is a comfy red and shiny pink.
It tastes like milky chocolate and juicy, red apples.
It smells like pink and red roses and lovely red strawberries.
It looks like joyful people on the silent streets and disco lights
                                                shining bright.
It sounds like children singing.
Love makes me happy.

Katie Rance (9)
St Mary Magdalene Catholic Primary School, Milton Keynes

Sorrow

Sorrow is cloudy grey and blank blue.
It smells like burning rubber and cut grass.
It looks like hurt children and old graves.
It sounds like heavy footsteps and plates smashing.
It tastes like burning hot water and stale bread.
Sorrow makes me feel *lonely*.

Katy Worton (9)
St Mary Magdalene Catholic Primary School, Milton Keynes

There Was A Young Boy Called Joe

There was a young boy called Joe,
Who sadly chopped off his left toe.
He leapt up into space,
You should have seen his face,
Then fell on the floor and said, *'Doh!'*

Erin Soden (9)
St Mary Magdalene Catholic Primary School, Milton Keynes

Autumn Is . . .

Autumn is a graceful and delicate girl in her glorious prime,
Grown from the tender child of summer,
She goes drifting across the land,
Turning the green leaves coffee-brown, ruby, amber and gold
And painting the countryside all her favourite colours.
The cooling night breeze is her peaceful breathing,
Calming the land as her tender slumber sweeps over us.
The shining moon in the pitch-black sky is her pale face
And her luscious, crimson cheeks are the ruby berries on
browning bushes.
Autumn sprays her fragrant perfume of toasted cinnamon,
Of poppies in full bloom and of rain over everything.
Her pearly tears of sorrow are the glinting drops of dew on a
spider's silken web.
Her whispery voice is the whip of the wind as it swerves in and out
of bare trees.
Her eyes are a pair of grey clouds, deep, dark and swirling.

This is magnificent autumn, a wondrous person and a terrific
season too.

Jessica Hipwell (10)
St Mary Magdalene Catholic Primary School, Milton Keynes

Sadness

Sadness is lightning-grey and black darkness.
It tastes like hunger and dirty water.
It smells like lonesome people in the night.
It looks like rain dripping on a stormy day.
It sounds like cries of children and low, sad speaking.
Sadness makes me cry.

Benita Cappellano (9)
St Mary Magdalene Catholic Primary School, Milton Keynes

Love

Love is bright pink and dark red.
It looks like a love heart and a joyful rose.
It sounds like people dancing and children singing.
It smells like a lovely rose and crunchy chocolate.
It tastes like hot chocolate and delicious food.
Love makes me *happy*.

Lauren Joy (9)
St Mary Magdalene Catholic Primary School, Milton Keynes

Love

Love is shining red and bright pink.
It tastes like sweet melons and melting toffees.
It smells like tasty marshmallows on a beautiful beach.
It looks like a blushing red rose and happy faces.
It sounds like feathery birds singing and happy laughing.
Love makes me *joyful!*

Maxwell Graham (9)
St Mary Magdalene Catholic Primary School, Milton Keynes

Love

Love is shiny red and sunset pink.
It tastes like runny chocolate on a hot, sunny evening.
It smells like freshly picked roses and violent scented perfume.
It looks like heavenly saints and angelic doves.
It sounds like complete, golden silence.
Love makes me *dream*.

Jordan Keating (9)
St Mary Magdalene Catholic Primary School, Milton Keynes

Anger

Anger is sweaty red and midnight-black.
It tastes like mouldy cheese and sour milk.
It smells like red-hot jelly on a hot day.
It looks like a fist being thrown in the air.
It sounds like ghosts howling at the moon.
Anger makes me *mad!*

Dylan Joseph (9)
St Mary Magdalene Catholic Primary School, Milton Keynes

Love

Love is sweet white and rosy red.
It tastes like beautiful hearts and gorgeous candy.
It smells like bubbly bath on a winter's day.
It looks like a shiny locket and a dreamy day.
It sounds like birds singing and gentle music.
Love makes me feel warm.

Joanna Lloyd Knibbs (9)
St Mary Magdalene Catholic Primary School, Milton Keynes

My Memory

It was about eleven days to a very special day
And that was my mum and dad's wedding day.
There were four page boys
And four flower girls.
We really enjoyed that day.

Nathaniel Graham (9)
St Mary Magdalene Catholic Primary School, Milton Keynes

Autumn's Child

Autumn is a little girl -
She smells of ripened fruit.
Her ruby cloak sends the summer away.
As she walks along the golden cornfields,
She bends over to pluck up some rich, golden corn
With bare twig fingers.

Her eyes are melted chocolate, so rich and creamy,
Her skin smells of cinnamon muffins.

She cuddles up to her mother to keep her warm and toasty.

Alice Davies (11)
St Mary Magdalene Catholic Primary School, Milton Keynes

The Moon

The moon is like a big snowball,
Soaring through the air.
It is like a big meatball,
Painted the colour white.

The moon is like a banana,
Floating in a dark space.
It is like a big tennis ball,
Flying through the air.

Danielle Lauderdale (8)
St Mary Magdalene Catholic Primary School, Milton Keynes

Jealousy

Jealousy is mucky green and gooey brown.
It tastes like bitter bananas and yucky bogies.
It smells like horrid sweat in a hot spit.
It looks like disgusting faces and total weirdness.
It sounds like tigers roaring and evil ghosts.

Jealousy makes me *scared!*

Sophie Guiry (9)
St Mary Magdalene Catholic Primary School, Milton Keynes

The Autumn Dragon

Autumn is a dragon burning the russet leaves with its hot,
scarlet breath.
Its sharp, bare, twig teeth crush summer as it sinks through
deep, rusty earth.
The birds migrate as rock-hard, conker-like droppings pepper
the trees.
Its amber scales reflect the honey sun onto the leaves,
Turning them into a dark autumn rainbow.
Its eyes glare a cold, hard stare at the destruction it has made.
It carries on until the dark winter knight slays it away.

Emilio Baqueiro (10)
St Mary Magdalene Catholic Primary School, Milton Keynes

Autumn Life

Autumn is a messy boy.
His friends are different colours crawling on the floor.
Autumn loves to sway, breathing air to the dusty music.
He sits near the radiator and hibernates.
His brown eyes go watery and sweep across the soil.
Before he goes to school, he gathers his food.
At the beginning of his birthday, he goes on holiday to Africa.
His face is a tangerine, pumpkin-round with a cornfield hairstyle.
He rubs his hands hard to keep the ants warm.
His sunshine face sleeps away in the afternoon.

Patricia Ogunjobi (10)
St Mary Magdalene Catholic Primary School, Milton Keynes

The Moon

The moon is like a silver town in the sky.
It is like a crystal ball floating in the sky.
It is like a glittery snowball.
The moon is like a silver banana moving from side to side.
The moon is like a silver plate flying through the air.

Yvette Boateng (8)
St Mary Magdalene Catholic Primary School, Milton Keynes

Autumn

Autumn is a housewife,
She clears up after her summer husband.
While her husband prepares for next summer,
She sews the patchwork fields.

She polishes conkers and wraps them up in spiky cases.
At night she polishes the moon,
Makes sure it's right
And places darkness so the moon is full, waxing or waning.

The rain is her tears.
She cries for her husband.
When morning comes she paints the leaves in autumn colours -
Crimson, amber and beige.

She lowers her misty net curtains.
She perfumes the trees
So they smell of cinnamon
And toasted wood.

Her eyes are large amber leaves,
Her nose is a chocolate-coloured pine cone,
She only has one wish . . .

She wants summer to come back.

Kate Hollins (9)
St Mary Magdalene Catholic Primary School, Milton Keynes

My Best Friend

My best friend
Is always lots of fun.
If I am told to do something
She will help until it's done.

If I am bored or lonely,
She will play with me.
I like to stay inside her flat
To sit and watch TV.

Mariah May Kelly (8)
St Mary Magdalene Catholic Primary School, Milton Keynes

Life Without My Best Friend

Without you:
I'm a city with no legend
Without you:
I'm a generation with no hero
Without you:
I'm a town with no myth
Without you:
I'm a house with no garden
Without you:
I'm a bird with no wings
Without you:
I'm a river with no breeze
Without you:
I'm a book with no words
Without you:
I'm a horse with no rider
Without you:
I'm a doctor with no patient.

Alyssa Adabie (9)
St Mary Magdalene Catholic Primary School, Milton Keynes

Memories

I had a cat, he ran away
I have a dog, a one-eyed dog
My first day at school
I had to wear a tie
My first day at school
I was very shy
On my first holy communion
I had bread and wine
We had a great day and
The weather was fine.

James Cochrane (9)
St Mary Magdalene Catholic Primary School, Milton Keynes

Autumn Is . . .

Autumn is a woman in her prime,
Throwing off her bright clothes of summer.
Her perfume is fresh cinnamon scent.
The falling, crackly leaves are her rotting teeth,
Dying with the bright colours of summer.
Her red-hot anger is the whooshing wind,
Blowing around the empty trees.
The blurry mist is her failing eyesight.
Her classic clothes of the new season
Are the beige, amber and honey-coloured leaves
That fall from the spiky autumn trees.
A rough pine cone is her shivery, shining nose.
Her long, lifeless hair is the dull, dry hay of harvest.
Her hacking cough is the loud, boisterous fireworks
In the autumn night.
The scarlet apples from harvest are her weathered, rosy cheeks.
Her longer, relaxing sleeps are the shorter autumn days.

Alice Rose (10)
St Mary Magdalene Catholic Primary School, Milton Keynes

Autumn Is . . .

Autumn is an excited young man,
Mischievously changing the weather of the colourful season.
His large, owl-like eyes are the puddles in the muddy ground.
He is wiping off the brightness of summer and pulling on the
blanket of winter.
He goes to sleep earlier and wakes up later.
His large footprints are the dark colours in the grey sky.
The wind is his child, surrounding him always.
He is covering the land with his favourite colours - red, orange
and brown.

His hair is the leaves that haven't fallen yet.
His body is the trunk.
His breath is the cold air on damp mornings.

Anna O'Hagan (10)
St Mary Magdalene Catholic Primary School, Milton Keynes

Autumn Is . . .

Autumn is a middle-aged woman
Putting on the colourful clothes of the new season

Her long, beautiful hair with shades of brown and red
Says farewell to their season

Autumn is a woman whose voice is the soft, gentle wind
Her quick walk is the leaves falling to the ground swiftly

Her scent is the perfume of poppies growing in the field
Her tears are the fresh, autumn rain growing into a savage storm

Her anger is the Hallowe'en night scary, terrifying and ghostly
Her smile lights up a thousand fireworks in the sky

Autumn is truly beautiful.

Lilian Harrison (10)
St Mary Magdalene Catholic Primary School, Milton Keynes

What Is Yellow?

Yellow is cheese, smelly and dairy.
Yellow is the sunset high in the sky.
Yellow is paint, dry and dark.
Yellow is the colour of someone's hair.
Yellow is the sun's bright light.
Yellow is the sand, soft and sprinkly.

Kirstie-Anne Woodman (7)
St Mary Magdalene Catholic Primary School, Milton Keynes

What Is Black?

Black is a spider creepy and crawly.
Black is a car, it's fast and can zoom.
Black is a pencil all coloured around the paper.
Black is a marker pen writing on the board.
Black is a computer nice and cool.
Black is a coat all smooth and nice.

Kirsten Perie (7)
St Mary Magdalene Catholic Primary School, Milton Keynes

Autumn Is . . .

Autumn is a gleaming and joyful girl in her delicate prime
Sweeping across the land with colours.
Her straightened, straw hair is the ploughed fields
In the distant meadows.
Heavy, ghostly breathing is the blustery winds
Cutting in and out the trees.
Her sparkling, sweeping eyelashes
Are falling leaves from the trees.
Rosy cheeks are the pink poppies blowing in the wind.
Her wrinkly nose is the fresh, darkened berries in the bushes.
Her fluffy, silken feet are the pale clouds in the autumn sky.
Her fresh, fond smile is a gleaming, ruby raspberry.

Kirby Haddon (10)
St Mary Magdalene Catholic Primary School, Milton Keynes

What Is Yellow?

Yellow is the smell of a big banana.
Yellow is the taste of butter on toast.
Yellow is the sight of loads of lights.
Yellow is the taste of wobbly jelly.
Yellow is the sight of the bright yellow sun.
Yellow is the smell of smelly cheese.
Yellow is the colour of the twinkling stars.
Can you imagine living without yellow?

Ratidzo Tapera (7)
St Mary Magdalene Catholic Primary School, Milton Keynes

What Is Black?

Black is night-time all shiny and bright.
Black is the tip of your pencil.
Black is the black ink on a typewriter.
Black is a zebra's stripes all stripy and white.
Black is the pavement when it is wet.

Elliot Giddins (7)
St Mary Magdalene Catholic Primary School, Milton Keynes

Autumn Is . . .

Autumn is a middle-aged man
Setting off fireworks of colour into the countryside.
Autumn is a middle-aged man
Painting his favourite colours, maroon, gold and beige.
His sorrowful tears are dazzling dew
Resting on the spider's silken, fragile web.
Pine cones are his crinkled nose.
Conkers are his eyes, round and shining in his face.
His spiky hair is the stubble of the cornfields.

Ben Miles (10)
St Mary Magdalene Catholic Primary School, Milton Keynes

What Is Blue?

Blue is the sky that shines up high.
Blue are the dolphins that jump up high.
Blue is the sea that swims up and down.
Blue are the fishes going up and around.
Blue are berries that are nice and sweet.
Blue are the raindrops that fall from the sky nice and neat.
They drop in your eyes and soak down your feet.

Jade Addai (7)
St Mary Magdalene Catholic Primary School, Milton Keynes

What Is Blue?

Blue is a beautiful blue robin.
Blue is the sky for a beautiful blue butterfly.
You can taste the blueberries.
The sea is rushing up and down and around.
The smell of the blue, beautiful violets and shining so bright.
Blue is the dolphin jumping so high.

Bethany McCann (7)
St Mary Magdalene Catholic Primary School, Milton Keynes

Autumn Is A Dog

Autumn is a dog
Chewing at the brass sun
His hair falls down as the leaves tumble
Side to side to the ground.

The nights grow darker
The dog shades his colour
Spiky trees are knots in his fur.

Patchwork fields are his dog's blanket
In a wicker basket
He barks at the birds
And the birds fly south in fear.

Connor Lauderdale (10)
St Mary Magdalene Catholic Primary School, Milton Keynes

What Is Grey?

Grey is a road that cars can drive over.
Grey is a dolphin that swims in the sea.
Grey is a cloud who tells us it's raining.
Grey is a sock that smells and stretches.
Grey is metal which tastes funny.

Nathan Merridan (8)
St Mary Magdalene Catholic Primary School, Milton Keynes

What Is Blue?

Blue is the sea, deep and wavy.
Blue is the sky, bright and moving.
Blue is the rain, hard and watery.
Blue are the raindrops, round and wet.
Blue is wallpaper, all scrunchy and torn.

Joshua Dean (7)
St Mary Magdalene Catholic Primary School, Milton Keynes

The Moon

The moon is like a snowflake
With glitter on it.
It looks like stars
But in a different shape.

The moon is like a bowling ball
Waiting for a strike.
It looks like your head
But with a bite.

The moon looks like cheese
But you cannot eat it.
You can't because
It has to move.

James Suter (7)
St Mary Magdalene Catholic Primary School, Milton Keynes

The Moon

The moon is like a disco ball
Glittering in the sky.
It's like a smiley face
Sleeping all day and night.

The moon is like a belly, fat
From eating too much Delight.
It's like a glittering picture
Flying in the night.

The moon is white like the sun
Flying like a snowball.
It's like a bunch of planets
Flying in north Mars.

Miraid Linehan (8)
St Mary Magdalene Catholic Primary School, Milton Keynes

The Moon

The moon is like a ball of snow
Thrown by an Eskimo.
It is like a big bowling ball
With lots of finger holes.

The moon glitters in the dark
Just like a disco ball.
It is like a person's brain
Spinning around getting very dizzy.

The moon is like a meteor
Flying backwards into space.

Alice Smith (8)
St Mary Magdalene Catholic Primary School, Milton Keynes

The Moon

The moon is like a white sun
A snowball gliding in the sky
A smiling banana
Against black sugar paper
The moon stands out amongst the beautiful
Broken glass stars
Shining brightly like a diamond
In a coal fire.

Jake Wingrove (8)
St Mary Magdalene Catholic Primary School, Milton Keynes

A Memory

When I went to Spain my brain was full of excitement
When we arrived it was very hot
We didn't have a car, we walked
We saw big houses owned by the rich
You could play lots of football on the pitch
My memories of Spain are made of happy, sunny times.

Sheridan O'Sullivan (8)
St Mary Magdalene Catholic Primary School, Milton Keynes

Autumn Days

I saw autumn passed today
With skin of ageing fruit.
It comes and goes but happily stays till bonfire smoke fades.
The frosty, dewy spiders' webs are nets of fisher-spider.
Its spiky trees and fireworks are a lovely bouquet.
When you wake up your eyes are a blue,
Your sight is covered with leaves of sleep.
Leaves fall and autumn sweeps them away
With its blustery winds.
Days shorten with cold stars
Falling on the fields.
Conkers are eyes waiting to open.

Victoria Bates (10)
St Mary Magdalene Catholic Primary School, Milton Keynes

Autumn's Spell

Autumn is a wizard
His hair wild and wavy: the colour a glorious maroon
He floats like falling leaves proudly into the newly formed season
He wears a golden cloak
His wand is a twig with no leaves
When he waves it
Twinkling stars fly
To the night sky
His magic ripens the fruit on the trees
And makes the world a magical place.

Lucy Freeman (11)
St Mary Magdalene Catholic Primary School, Milton Keynes

The Moon

The moon makes the darkness bright on the darkest night.
The moon is like a snowball soaring through the air.
The moon spins day and night, it never stops.

Luke Gardner (7)
St Mary Magdalene Catholic Primary School, Milton Keynes

Autumn

Autumn is the grandad of the year,
His toasted beard is a sparkly crimson and russet
Bonfires are burning in his eyes
Sending the scent of smoky stubble
The ochre-coloured trees are tinged with tangerine
The grandad's breath sends a coat of mist all over the sky.
Grandad tells us autumn stories that have passed.
He hugs us in the September sun
And hands us the fruit of autumn days.

Christian Alifoe (10)
St Mary Magdalene Catholic Primary School, Milton Keynes

My Holiday

When I got on the plane
All I could think about
Was getting to Spain.
When I got there the
Sun was so strong
I could not stay in it
For very long. I could
Not wait to jump in the
Pool to make me very cool.

Sam James Botham (9)
St Mary Magdalene Catholic Primary School, Milton Keynes

What Is Red?

What is red? Flames of burning fire are red.
What is red? A ladybird is red.
What is red? Tomato ketchup is very tasty.
What is red? Roses are red, smelling as good as perfume.
What is red? Beautiful red cars, that zoom up and down the motorway.
What is red? Lips are red when you smile and say hello.
What is red? A big, juicy apple.

Andre Bird (8)
St Mary Magdalene Catholic Primary School, Milton Keynes

Missing You

Without you I'm like a toe with no nails,
A city with no lights.
Like a pitch with no players or a garden without snails.

Without you I'm like a book with no pages,
A bike with no wheels.
Like a pod with no peas or a tree with no branches.

Without you I'm like a rose with no petals,
A bottle with no water.
Like a branch with no leaves or a factory with no metals.

Without you I'm like a ruler with no numbers,
A name with no letters.
Like pencil with no lead or a facial with no cucumber.

Olivia Easden (8)
St Mary Magdalene Catholic Primary School, Milton Keynes

What Is Red?

What is red? Roses are red
Roses for me, roses for you.
Ladybirds are red and tickle you.
Berries are red and good to eat.
They are so good to eat it doesn't
Make you speak.
Apples are red too and shiny as well.
They are juicy and I love the smell.
Robins are red as well, they fly in the sky.
And they are as red as flames and they love to fly.

Marco Palmieri (8)
St Mary Magdalene Catholic Primary School, Milton Keynes

What Is Yellow?

What is yellow?
Lions are yellow
Running through the jungle.
Stars are yellow
Sparkling in the night.
Wheat is yellow
All along the fields.
Sand is yellow
Spraying around the desert.
Fire is yellow
And you can dance around it.
The sun is yellow
And fiery each new day.
Bees are yellow
Buzzing all around you.

Niamh O'Hanlon (9)
St Mary Magdalene Catholic Primary School, Milton Keynes

Why?

Why is the sky so high?
Why is the ground so low?
Why do cats purr?
Why do dogs woof?
Why do fish swim?
Why is the grass green?
Why is water clear?
Why is the world so beautiful?
I really do not know.

Catherine Suter & Katie O'Hagan (8)
St Mary Magdalene Catholic Primary School, Milton Keynes

What Is White?

What is white? Doves are white
Fluttering in the white sky.
What else is white? Swans are white
Gliding on the pond or lake.
Sugar is white too,
So tasty sugar is
Snow,
Nothing wrong with snow,
So delicate you can't get enough.
Milk is white, good for your white bones too.
The moon is white,
Lights up the dark sky.
I just love white.

Adrian Soden (9)
St Mary Magdalene Catholic Primary School, Milton Keynes

Bonfire Memories

Stars crackle,
Leaves burn,
Fire gleams,
Now it is the fireworks' turn
Up and around
Down to the ground
Jump up high
Into the sky!
People scream as the rockets are seen,
Going *weeee bom!*
With their own song.

Sarah Gatley (10)
St Mary Magdalene Catholic Primary School, Milton Keynes

Green

Green is the colour of crispy cabbage and lovely celery,
Green is the colour of a satisfying, juicy pear,
Green is the colour of the prickly cactus and the crunchy lettuce,
Green is the colour of a sweet grape in your mouth,
Green is the colour of the wet grass in the morning,
Green is the colour of toads and frogs
Leaping on the lily pads in a pond,
Green is the colour of a grasshopper
Hopping around on a sunny day.

Isabella Arionget (8)
St Mary Magdalene Catholic Primary School, Milton Keynes

Darkness

The church bells were singing in the moonlight
The creepy old house was full of spiders.
The sound of an owl in the background
The trees blew in the wind outside
While inside people were scared.
Rats ran round their feet and spiders crawled up their legs.
The family was unhappy
Because of sharing their homes with unwanted guests.
Outside the gates slammed together like hands clapping.

Telsey Stimpson (10)
Simpson School, Milton Keynes

The Dark Night

In the dark night there stood a house
In the dark night quiet as a mouse
The shadow spread across the ground
The night listened for a sound
The trees stood like soldiers
Their roots held them in the ground.

Jaque De Baugy (10)
Simpson School, Milton Keynes

Freedom

Listen to the bell sing loudly
Watch the owls soar through the sky
Wonder what it would be like to be a tree
Ask yourself what would you like to be
Look at the gate standing proud in the light
Look at the house shimmer at night
See the moon reflect on the path
Hear Big Ben chanting away
And wish that you would be free
Look at the wall crack a smile
The lights are still on but the man has gone.

Derryn Hudson (10)
Simpson School, Milton Keynes

Pitch-Black Midnight

The moon stared silently.
The gates rattled quietly.
The owls hooted proudly.
The stiff, stone wall stood angrily.
The tree twisted round and about
As the clock moaned through the night.

Jodie Towell (10)
Simpson School, Milton Keynes

The Misty Night

The church bells rang,
As the moon shone bright above the mysterious house,
The gate stood silently and still.
The trees tried to touch one another,
The house slept, worriedly waiting for his owner.

Hibak Jama (10)
Simpson School, Milton Keynes

The Mysterious Mansion

The house stands in the middle of the city.
A woman called Mary lives there.
The moon looks down every night.
The owl watches from the iron entrance.
The church bells shout across the city.
The rusty gate stands silently at the front.
Bang! The door shuts as if it was racing and hit a tree.

Khama Banda (10)
Simpson School, Milton Keynes

The Haunted Town

Trees standing like huge guards.
The spooky house moaning for his old owner.
Bells ringing but no one is there.
The moon frowned over the haunted town.

Callum Spray (10)
Simpson School, Milton Keynes

The Moon

The moon eats up the darkness.
The moon skips across the sky
Smiling brightly as Big Ben sings beautifully
As the moon falls asleep.

Vicki Vernon (10)
Simpson School, Milton Keynes

The Old House

The spooky old house full of hairy spiders.
There were bats, rats and mice in an old house
Also a ghost and a cat.

Scott Culley (10)
Simpson School, Milton Keynes

The Mansion Of The Night

The gate standing like an iron soldier protecting the mansion.
The tree reaching to the window sill trying to get in.
The shadows running across the drive.
The moon shining like an eye in the mist.
The chimneys crossing like a man on the roof.
The bushes like faces in the night.
The lights from the mansion like eyes looking for the owner,
Never returned.

Kalhun Carr (10)
Simpson School, Milton Keynes

A Night In London

The moon lit up the ground like a gem.
The church bells sang loudly across the city like a choir.
The cold, frozen gate stood like a soldier.
The branches reached out for a friend.
An owl sat on the scary iron gate like stone.
The house crept back from the night.
The stiff wall stood in the shadows guarding the house.
The windows lit up as the clock struck midnight.

Jordan Noon (10)
Simpson School, Milton Keynes

A Spooky Night

The moon glowed while watching the trees waving.
Singing in the shadows.
The stone, stiff wall stood guarding its territory.
The owl hooted in the misty shadows of the night.
The clock scrunched up its face and turned away.
The church bells chimed throughout the city.
The haunted house stood in the guardianship of the moon.
The windows lit up when the clock struck midnight.

Rhiannon Fox (10)
Simpson School, Milton Keynes

Environment

When I went on my holiday I could see
Roller coasters and dolphins getting fed.
I could see sharks in the aquarium,
I could see alligators in the lake,
I could see castles and fireworks,
I could also see Mickey and Minnie
With all the other Disney characters.

I could feel the dolphin's smooth skin on my hands,
I could feel the boiling sun on my skin,
I could feel the breeze against my skin,
I could feel the water against my face.

Chloe Duff (9)
Simpson School, Milton Keynes

Environment

When I went on my holiday,
I saw a lot of things,
You would not believe what I felt.
My body went into a backflip,
While swinging on the swings.
I really don't know what I saw,
But I do know I heard something.
I think I heard relatives screaming
On a roller coaster while waving and singing.

Danielle Harrison (9)
Simpson School, Milton Keynes

I Can See . . .

I can see
Big, fast aeroplanes
In the sky.
They zoom over my head.

Joshua Clements (9)
Simpson School, Milton Keynes

On The Way To School

As I walk along the pavement
Speedy sports car races in front.
A colourful spider in its web.
I get caught on spiky bushes
And the rough bark of the trees.
I always hear that yellow digger.
The sound of magpies.
Children rushing worriedly to school.
Five minutes later we arrive at school
Then into the playground
Time for another day at school.

Tyler Cutts (8)
Simpson School, Milton Keynes

Environment

I can see the people playing in the snow
And they are jumping up and down
And trees letting go of the leaves.
I can feel the dew and animals running round my feet
And lots of warm bread.
I can hear the busy street and people running round
And my mum coming home from work.

Gabrielle Jane Beasley (10)
Simpson School, Milton Keynes

Environment

I am seeing the busy streets of New York,
The other strangers digging in dustbins for food,
Tourists taking photos.
I can feel people knocking me to get past,
I feel nervous as I get on the plane,
I feel my dad giving me a hug and my mum as well.
I can hear police sirens pounding in my eardrum.

Kelly Nicole Hutson (9)
Simpson School, Milton Keynes

On My Way To School

As Mum and I drive down the street,
We hear the rushing and clattering of feet.
There are church bells ringing,
Blackbirds singing.
In through the gates we go,
Squirrels scurrying up trees,
Chatty parents walking slow.
My warm coat keeps me safe from the breeze.
At last it's time to start a long school day.
A hug for Mum and so now I am on my way!

Elizabeth Mulcahy (8)
Simpson School, Milton Keynes

On My Way To School

I see children rushing with their parents
And leaves falling from the trees.
I hear cars zooming down the road,
Squirrels scampering up trees.
I feel the cold air rushing past my hand,
The rain is pattering on my umbrella.
Finally I arrived at school.
Could today be one when I won't act the fool?

Arthur Woolley (8)
Simpson School, Milton Keynes

Silent, Misty Night

The tree stretched its giant hands.
The moon's round face looked over the house.
The house's eyes glowed in the misty darkness.
The clock stood watch protecting the town.
Cobwebs blew in the wind like silver hair.

Ciaran Clark (10)
Simpson School, Milton Keynes

Sherlock Holmes

The moon smiles upon the haunted house.
Before you go in you try to open the gate
But you can't get in.
The trees are the soldiers of the house
But no one knows that except Sherlock Holmes.
Stone walls and some girl
Finds a way into the lodge of Sherlock Holmes.
She goes onto the roof.
This girl has a pair of glasses on.
There is a massive bell going off.
The girl wears a hairband on her head.
The rusty steel gate stands strong at the entrance.
It is climbed by the girl.
The garden is haunted by the trees
Because they were the soldiers.
The house isn't any old house, it is a lodge.

Corey Ringer (10)
Simpson School, Milton Keynes

War

I can see . . .
The bombs making the explosion,
The fire burning the children,
The planes shooting at the buildings.

I can feel . . .
The blood dripping down my arm,
My arm getting burnt,
The coldness of my gun.

I can hear . . .
The missile rush as I'm running home,
The children screaming for help,
The bullet going through my tummy.

Kristina Kent-Rettig (9)
Simpson School, Milton Keynes

In The Playground

P eople chatting on the decking
L aying down on the dry, grassy hill
A nd lots of people playing games
Y apping and chatting loudly
G rowing lots of seeds from a packet for new grass
R olling down the wet, muddy hill
O n the playground lots of people are getting tagged
U nderstanding lots of people's needs
N ew people playing on the playground
D oing lots of things in it is always lots of fun.

Dane Morgan (9)
Simpson School, Milton Keynes

Hallowe'en

H allowe'en is spooky.
A ll the people are dressing up.
L ights are off.
L anterns are showing.
O n Hallowe'en it's scary tonight.
W hen people are happy it's on Hallowe'en.
E veryone loves Hallowe'en.
E veryone goes round knocking.
N o one is unhappy on Hallowe'en.

Gemma Argent (9)
Simpson School, Milton Keynes

War

I can see my campfire,
I can feel anger coming to me,
I can hear cars going past.

Jamielee Tucker Spiers (9)
Simpson School, Milton Keynes

Autumn And Hallowe'en Are Nice

Autumn is nice
Roll the dice
Leaves are falling
And babies are crawling.

Lines on leaves,
They all believe,
The wind blew
And my dream came true.

On Hallowe'en
People are mean,
Going up and down the street,
They knock on doors and say, 'Trick or treat?'

Sarah Roberts (10)
Simpson School, Milton Keynes

Autumn

Winter is coming
Leaves are changing
The harvest fayre
The trees are bare.

Snow may fall
While babies crawl.
My wish came true
While the wind blew.

On Hallowe'en they're so mean
Trick or treat
Smell my feet
Or give me something good to eat.

Saffron Lucas (9)
Simpson School, Milton Keynes

Environment

I can see bugs on a leaf
And my mum stirring up potatoes,
People walking in shops,
People driving on the motorway.
I can feel my hand reaching to eat a chocolate bar,
My hairs standing on my back as I walk out of my door.
I can hear opera singers sing,
Birds twittering in the trees,
The wind whistling in the trees.
I can feel my cosy bed as I climb into it.

Wesley Brown (9)
Simpson School, Milton Keynes

On My Way To School

On my way to school
As I walked along the path to my school
I saw a little cat climbing a tree.
As I walked along the street
There was a black and white cow
Eating grass in the fields.
I heard a loud banging at the next door neighbour's house.
I heard a baby crying upstairs in its bedroom.
I felt very sad about my sick dog.
I felt very happy about me and my friends.

Charlyn Kumadi (9)
Simpson School, Milton Keynes

Bullies

Bullies are horrid
Bullies are sly
They often kick you
And make you cry.

Alice Walker (7)
Weedon Bec Primary School, Northampton

A Bully

A big, bad bully is nothing but trouble
Always bursting everyone's bubble
A bully is a nasty thing
A bully thinks he's the king
A bully will bite
A bully will fight
A bully really isn't that bright.

A bully isn't nice
A bully is mean
A bully hates adults knowing that he's mean
A bully takes lunch money
A bully draws a long line down your work
A bully thinks he's the boss.

A bully pushes people over
A bully lies all the time
I hate bullies
So you should tell.

Emily Conder (7)
Weedon Bec Primary School, Northampton

A Big Bully

A scary bully came up to me.
The bully was big.
I was afraid of the big bully.
The bully went, I was on my own.
I kept shivering.
I told my mummy and daddy.
They went out to see who did it.
I felt safe.

India Daniels (7)
Weedon Bec Primary School, Northampton

Friends

F riends are lots of fun
R unning around and playing with me
I like to play
E ach friend is special
N aughty and good
D ays are better with friends
S o we'll be friends forever!

Alice Bendy (8)
Weedon Bec Primary School, Northampton

A Bully

B ig, fat and ugly,
U nfair, scared, silly and selfish,
L olly stealers, smelly and freaky,
L azy, unkind and creepy,
I really hate bullies,
E vil spirit,
S o if you get *bullied* go and tell.

Joseph Gilbert (7)
Weedon Bec Primary School, Northampton

Summertime

S ummer is when the sun shines.
U p, up, the sun is in the sky.
M osaics of yellow in the sky.
M aybe there will be a rainbow.
E choes coming from the sea, the sun is shining, come and play
with me.
R ainbows, rainbows, right up in the blue sky.

Alexandra Holyoak (9)
Weedon Bec Primary School, Northampton

Super Girl!

S he's brilliant and speedy
U nderneath she is quite greedy
P erhaps I'll ask her to come and play?
E rm, I wonder which day?
R ight, it'll be on Saturday

G reat . . . I'll give her a teddy bear
I wonder what to wear?
R ed dress, pink shoes
L ight or dark? How can I choose?

Calvin Thorogood (8)
Weedon Bec Primary School, Northampton

Football

F ootball is my favourite game
O ther sports just aren't the same
O n Saturdays I watch them play
T o see them score home or away
B est of all are the Gunners
A lways are the fastest runners
L jungberg is better than all the rest
L ose or win they're still the best.

Ashley Rawlings (9)
Weedon Bec Primary School, Northampton

Haunt

H allowe'en, the night of haunting
A re you scared of the ghosts?
U ntold danger around the village
N ight-time horrors when you go to bed
T ime to *beware!*

Jessica Browne (9)
Weedon Bec Primary School, Northampton

Bullies

I hate bullies
They are mean
They make me cry
They're silly
They're not kind
They make me feel sad and lonely
I would help my friends if they were bullied.
Would you?

Colleen Hogan (7)
Weedon Bec Primary School, Northampton

Bullies

Bullies shout
I am lonely
She isn't letting me play or talk
I can tell
I can walk away
I can tell some adults
And now I feel much better.

Cally Brooks (7)
Weedon Bec Primary School, Northampton

Bullies

Big, strong and unafraid
They run away from Mum
Because they don't like to be told off
I went to tell my mum
And she told them off.

Alice Sayward (7)
Weedon Bec Primary School, Northampton

Bullies!

Bullies are really mean to people
People can be really scared of bullies
The bullies are nasty to really kind people
Bullies take nice, good or best things
Bullies are really bad
Bullies are mean
I hate them so much
Bullying is bad
Bullies shout at people
I feel sad, upset and sorry for those who have been shouted at
People can walk away from the bullies.

Chelsea Marks (7)
Weedon Bec Primary School, Northampton

All About Me

Mischievous child
And funny too
Naughty sometimes
Tough too
I have lots of friends
End of me and my friends
And now we are back together again.

Samantha Nicholls-Kidner (9)
Weedon Bec Primary School, Northampton

A Bully

Nasty, horrible, can't count on them
Utterly mean and selfish
Calling names like pins in your heart
You just can't get away.

Georgina Holyoak (7)
Weedon Bec Primary School, Northampton

Bullying

Bullying is horrible
Please stop
Please, please
It is always terrifying
Go and tell an adult
Bullies do not like adults
If an adult does not come
Just run away
Bullies do not like adults
If an adult does not come
Just run away.

Laura Smith (7)
Weedon Bec Primary School, Northampton

Bullies!

Terrified, scared and upset,
No one to speak to,
So alone and so sad,
On your own,
I have to do what he said.

Francesca Sorrentino (7)
Weedon Bec Primary School, Northampton

A Bully

Bullies are scary
Shouting bullies are loud
Bullies are strong
And selfish
I don't like bullies.

Rhys Watkins (7)
Weedon Bec Primary School, Northampton

Football Crazy

Football crazy,
Football mad,
I have no other interests,
But that's not bad!

I wake up in the morning,
Football's always in my head,
One day I'll play for England,
Well, that's what Dad said!

I train all day,
I train all night,
So I will be the best,
Kicking balls against the walls,
And I never need a rest!

On Saturdays I play a match,
I'm on the winning team,
I tackle, I shoot, the ball's in the net,
The crowd lets out a scream!

I do not foul, I do not cheat,
I'm great up in the air,
They say that matched with Rooney,
We would be a cracking pair!

Dominic Knight (9)
Weedon Bec Primary School, Northampton

I Love My Violin

I love my violin
I pluck it
I fiddle it
I tuck it in its case
And kiss it goodnight
I love my violin
My sweet violin.

Rhiannon Kay (8)
Weedon Bec Primary School, Northampton

Adrenalin Rush!

When I'm speeding down that track,
That's what I call an adrenalin rush!
When I reach one hundred and up,
That's what I call an adrenalin rush!
When I zoom down the quarter-mile track,
That's what I call an adrenalin rush!
When I press that nitrous plunge,
That's what I call an adrenalin rush!
And now here I am racing up high,
Over my contenders, just passing by
And here comes the finish like a snap
And now the adrenalin rush has gone like that.

Mark Fennell (10)
Weedon Bec Primary School, Northampton

The Old Times
(It is about my real mother)

She was a loving mother
But now she is six feet under
She will always be in my heart and soul
Until I'm very old or six feet under too.

Austin Wilde (11)
Weedon Bec Primary School, Northampton

The Sea

I can see the sea
Splashing and crashing
Children screaming
In the caves are beaming
I can see the sea.

Alex Horner (9)
Weedon Bec Primary School, Northampton

My Favourite Room In My House

My bedroom is my private place
Even my parents cannot invade this space
When my friends come around
We may even dress up in a gown

Even though it may be late
We may even get to eat some chocolate
Then it is time to go to sleep
My friends and I will count some sheep

In the morning when the day is dawning
We are awoken and will start yawning
By the pigeons on the roof
Oh my goodness, we are aloof

My parents are first up out of their nest
And get up to make our breakfast
When we are washed and ready for play
It's time for my friends to go home and make hay.

Hannah Barnes (8)
Weedon Bec Primary School, Northampton

Christmas

Winter is very cold
And the leaves turn gold.
When the children come out to play
They hang their coats on Christmas Day
When they're home every day on winter holidays.
Come! Christmas is nearly here,
Better see the reindeers.
Christmas lights everywhere,
On the trees and in the air.
Snowflakes fall from above,
I'm sending you lots of Christmas love.

Jorja Mills (8)
Weedon Bec Primary School, Northampton

Miller

Miller is my dog.
He always jumps at friends
When they come to play.

He sits on us before school.
When I come home
He wants to play ball.

We got him from a rescue shelter
And he had been there a week.
Now that he lives with us
He loves to eat apples.

He always pulls us down the hill
But he never pulls us up again.
He barks when we go out
And when we come back.

He absolutely loves the fuss
And never lets us go.
He likes to take post out of the letterbox
But never gives it to us.

Miller is such a lovely dog.
He never bites or snaps.
This makes me realise how lucky I am
That Miller is my dog.

Georgina Laye (9)
Weedon Bec Primary School, Northampton

Smile

S ee people smiling about happy thoughts,
M y favourite word that only I can adore,
 I share my smile all around, laughing is such a happy sound,
L et us be happy and wear the smile,
E veryone smile, don't hold it in, please smile at me, come,
   join in, *smile*.

Lauren Gilbert (9)
Weedon Bec Primary School, Northampton

My Little Sister

'M ummy, Mummy,'
Y ells my little sister

L ittle brat's telling on me again
I haven't done anything this time
T his always happens
T ugging at my hair
L ittle brat's
E ver so annoying

S queals when I pinch her on the arm
I 'm in terrible trouble now
S tomping up the stairs is Mum
T earful eyes look at me
'E nough!' shouts Mum
R eally we love each other very much.

Kayleigh Marks (10)
Weedon Bec Primary School, Northampton

Did Anyone Shed A Tear?

Hitler killed himself
Did anyone shed a tear?
No, cos we didn't care

Hitler had millions killed
Did anyone shed a tear?
Yes, cos we cared

Millions of Jews were killed
Did anyone shed a tear?
Yes, cos we cared

At dawn, June 6 '44,
The largest invasion you ever saw
Did anyone shed a tear?
Yes, cos we cared.

Courtney Hogan (9)
Weedon Bec Primary School, Northampton

The Bulldozer

There once was a magnificent garden
With different varieties of extravagant and exotic flowers
In rows of all the colours in the rainbow.
Occasionally there are beautiful showers,
As they fall they look like glittery crystals.

But one night
Where the showers look like broken glass
Darting towards you,
Where the headlights of the unexpected bulldozer
Are blindingly bright,
It comes charging through the garden
Trampling every living thing in sight.
Vroom, vroom, crushhh!
Oh no, Mr Driver, why are you coming towards me?

Emmah Suhail (10)
Weedon Bec Primary School, Northampton

Today's Forecast

Thunder and lightning
Is frightening,
Wind and air
Goes through my hair,
Ice and snow,
On my sledge I go,
Warmth and sun,
Everybody's having fun,
Rain and fog
While walking through a bog,
Weather comes and goes
Just like wind blows.

Amy Pask (10)
Weedon Bec Primary School, Northampton

Autumn Days

It's cold now in autumn,
The grass is all dewed,
The conkers are falling,
In the car park at school
The leaves are crunching
Under my feet
And ants are marching to the beat
Because now it's winter
And it's getting very cold
So it's tea and biscuits for all that are old.

Daniella Day (9)
Weedon Bec Primary School, Northampton

Red Rays

Red rays fire in all directions
NASA space shuttles fly
Trying to destroy the vast
Black aliens.
Meteorites go crashing by
Smashing defenceless space buggies.
The space station stands motionless
On its guard
As if not part of this battle.
What has happened to our world?
Where are all the people -
The towns,
The cities,
The old cottage down the lane?
No cars,
No buses,
Nothing,
Just bricks and dirt.
This is what's come to pass
Upon the once vital world
Called Earth.

Alex Freeman-Hall (9)
Wellingborough Preparatory School, Wellingborough

Christ On The Cross

Murky clouds linger
In the shadowy sky
Where His body has been crucified
With nails sharp as Hell,
That kind and honest man.
With His holed healing hands.
As one vicar prays
Another wonders,
Is He doing this for me?
But as we all know
He died to forgive our sins.
His blood,
    Drop
    By
    Drop
Stained the grass
Where He last stepped
And we remember Jesus Christ
Our Lord.

Issy Tai (10)
Wellingborough Preparatory School, Wellingborough

Whale Song

The whale glides through the ocean
Singing its beautiful song.
It ploughs
Through
Gently, softly
The waves tumbling, swishing, swashing
Above its head.
It smoothly swoops and plunges
Down into the deep
    Dark
       Depths.

Max Armstrong (10)
Wellingborough Preparatory School, Wellingborough

Judgement Day

I heard them coming
Through the town
I knew it was Judgement Day
Thousands of them clomping
Along the cobbles

The smoky smell of gunpowder
Filling the summer breeze
Our house was stormed
And we were dragged out
Like dogs to our golden green hills

Bodies stacked up ten high
And all through our meadows
And inside our town walls people getting killed
The smell of hate struck me
The children flinging their arms around their parents

Most of the townsfolk had been murdered
The rest of us knew
It would be our turn soon

I was beckoned forward
The acrid smell of gunpowder grew stronger
The cries grew louder
And it was over

Now as I look back
Through the mists of time
On that massacre
I feel a strange sadness
Like no other.

Alex Lill (10)
Wellingborough Preparatory School, Wellingborough

Hunkapi

(I am (related to everyone))

We stand between the mountains and the earth
Looking down upon our tranquil plains
Herds of buffalo graze in peace
God's great creation born free in harmony

The hawk soars up high
To be at one with the wind
Iyuptala is his cry
Echoing over the valley

Across the prairie we ride
The Itancan of our tribe
To the rushing river we journey
Flowing with life over ancient stones

Makataime Shekiakiak's tribe are the Saux
Born free, made slaves by history
The prayers and dreams of a nation wronged
Are carried on the winds of time.

Key
(Cherokee language)
Iyuptala (ee-yoo-Γ'THAT-lah) = to be at one with
Itancan (ee-THAN-chun) = leader of the herd
(Saux language)
Makataime Shekiakiaks = Black hawk

Ralph Titmuss (11)
Wellingborough Preparatory School, Wellingborough

The Triumph Of Death

The time has come,
It's Judgement Day,
A hunt for all the sinners
For whom the deadly bell tolls.

For gamblers *ding-dong*
For drunkards *ding-dong*
Adulterous lovers *ding-dong* and
Robbers *ding-dong*.

The gate to Hell is open,
The wrongdoers are tumbling in
Being pushed by the dead;
The Grim Reaper too.

The drumbeat is getting faster by the second.
Dead bodies litter the ground,
Even the king bites the dust
Trying to take all his riches.

Can you escape the scythe
That reaps your life?
Will you go to the gallows
Perused by fiendish monsters?

The time has come,
It's Judgement Day.

Charlie Oliver Miller (10)
Wellingborough Preparatory School, Wellingborough

Brother And Sister

A little boy, a big girl, will always get in a twirl.
Can't stop them any way!
An angry dad will scream and shout, but will that work?
Can't stop them any way!
A kind mum will give them things, but will that work?
Can't stop them any way!
A big, fat uncle comes to stay, but will that work?
Can't stop them any way!
A sick old grandad tells them a story, but will that stop them?
Can't stop them any way!
A friend stays round, but will that stop them?
Can't stop them any way!
A teacher dies, someone cries, but will that stop them?
Can't stop them any way!
A big, fat stranger gives them sweets . . .
That's the only way.

William Aitken (11)
Wellingborough Preparatory School, Wellingborough

Café Bizarre

In the room:
Lingering smell of cigarette smoke,
The rough table littered
With glass as cold as ice,
The clashing of cutlery and crockery,
The TV blazing cricket results.
The girls, like vampires,
Have sucked the blood from the man,
And divided him between them.

Rory Millett (11)
Wellingborough Preparatory School, Wellingborough

The Dragon

People say St George saved a princess
From being gobbled by a dragon.
But how do we know he was saving her
From its horrid, dragon breath?

I mean, she could have been having
A meal with the dragon, or playing,
Or maybe even dating!
If that's the case George is a murderer!

Maybe, somehow, it was related
To the Royal Family
And deserved to be king
More than George.

I believe as soon as he saw
The dragon's smug grin
He would have killed it anyway.
I believe St George was a fraud.

Ben Squire (10)
Wellingborough Preparatory School, Wellingborough

Alliteration Astronomy

Colourful collisions caused the cosmos where
Airless astronauts are abandoned
Plentiful, purple planets perform plays in
Silent, starlit skies whilst
Shining, shooting stars startle
Massive, menacing meteors who
Anxiously await aliens.

Lydia Smart (9)
Wellingborough Preparatory School, Wellingborough

I Shall Save The Universe

Bad things happen and we are really sad
We care but you are you and I am me
We listen to the news
We are lucky we are free.

Imagine we were slaves
Working for no pay
We would be very hungry
Especially at the end of the day.

Fighting and suffering are all around us
Imagine we were at war
We could escape the suffering
We couldn't if we were poor.

I would stop all the suffering
No wars, no slaves
I would make new homes for them
Far away across the waves.

Please do not worry
I have it all in hand
We come to school to learn
We'll be safe across the land.

Ruth Simone Sherry (8)
Wellingborough Preparatory School, Wellingborough